TALKING
WITH GOD

TALKING
WITH GOD

CHARLES
STANLEY

THOMAS NELSON PUBLISHERS
Nashville • Atlanta • London • Vancouver

Published in Nashville, Tennessee, by Thomas Nelson, Inc., Publishers, and distributed in Canada by Word Communications, Ltd., Richmond, British Columbia, and in the United Kingdom by Word (UK), Ltd., Milton Keynes, England.

Scripture quotations are from the NEW KING JAMES VERSION of the Bible. Copyright © 1979, 1980, 1982, Thomas Nelson, Inc., Publishers.

ISBN 0-7852-7276-3

Printed in the United States of America

CONTENTS

CONTENTS

INTRODUCTION

OUR NEED TO COMMUNICATE WITH GOD

Each of us has a need to communicate with God. That need has been built into us by our Creator. It is part of God's design—part of His putting His imprint on our lives. We *desire* to be in touch with our Maker.

Prayer is communication with God. In its broadest definition, prayer includes both verbal and nonverbal communication—it covers our thoughts and actions toward God, as well as our words toward God.

From this definition, some people may conclude that we are continually in communication with God because virtually everything that we do in our lives is a message that we send to God or make before God. After all, God sees everything we do and knows everything we think and feel. From this viewpoint, our entire lives are prayers of a sort.

Others may conclude that we live continually in an atmosphere of prayer because God is always communicating with us. He consistently sends us messages about His great love for us—we not only have the Bible as His Word, but messages in nature, messages that come through the loving actions and words of other people, and messages that we perceive in the deep stirring of our spirits.

These two views of prayer, however, are in error on one key point: *communication is a two-way process.* Simply sending a message is not communication. Communication requires that two parties respond to each other. Each party gives and receives messages and, in turn, provides feedback. In other words:

- A statement is made, and a specific response is provided.
- A question is asked, and an answer is given.
- Feelings are vented, and feelings are perceived in return.

True communication with God is not talking *to* God, but talking *with* God. We do not communicate if we voice a petition to God but do not wait for His answer. We do not communicate if we express our desires to God but do not hear what His desires are for us. We do not communicate if we vent our anger, frustration, doubt, fear, or joy to God but do not listen intently for His response.

Prayer is speaking to *and* listening to God. It is an active process involving two communicators: you and God.

Prayer Is Intentional

Prayer does not happen by accident. While we may express our prayers through feelings and thoughts, prayer must be intentional for it truly to be a form of communication. We must actively engage in the process. We must turn our minds and hearts and voices toward God.

Voicing a concern about a problem to a friend is not prayer. Silently wishing something might be so is not prayer. Confessing a fault to another person is not prayer. Feeling a spring in our step as we rejoice in the warmth and beauty of an April day is not prayer.

To be engaged in prayer, we must voice our problem to God . . . with an expectation that He not only will hear us but will respond to us.

To be engaged in prayer, we must yield our desires to God . . . and expect Him to answer or change our desires as part of the process.

To be in genuine prayer, we must make our confessions to God . . . and actively receive His cleansing and forgiveness.

To be people of prayer, we not only must feel positive, good, or thankful, but must give voice to our thanksgivings and praise . . . and open ourselves fully to experience the presence of God at work both in and around us.

Prayer Is Dialogue

From time to time, God may give us a directive or speak a command to us. Indeed, God speaks when He wills to speak, and it is our responsibility to listen and obey. We also voice to God our heartfelt cries of anguish, sorrow, pain, or give vent to our ecstatic joy. At these times we are talking to God or He is talking to us. This is *expression*, which is valuable, but it is not the most beneficial form of communication in a relationship.

Communication that builds relationships is dialogue. Genuine prayer has all of the qualities and characteristics of a deeply meaningful conversation between two people. God said to the prophet Isaiah, "Come now, and let us reason together" (Isa. 1:18). This image of God and man sitting down together for a good talk is our best image of prayer.

Can you imagine living in a relationship with a person who made demands or requests, or stated opinion or facts, but never waited to hear what you had to say? Such a relationship would be very unfulfilling. You might establish a degree of civility and function with a modicum of efficiency with that person, but the relationship would probably be very cold and unsatisfying to you.

That is precisely the nature of many people's prayer life. There is no heart to their communication with God, no real intimacy, and no deep fulfillment. For communication to be satisfying, it must involve a genuine dialogue, not a series of short monologues.

The end results of intentional dialogue can be wonderful. We know this to be true in our relationships with other people. When we have a deep and heartfelt conversation with another person, we very often come away from that experience saying, "I have a much better understanding of him and his problems, needs, and concerns," "I have deeper feelings toward that person," "I have a greater appreciation for who she is," or "We have a stronger friendship."

The same is true when we communicate intentionally and in dialogue with God. We know Him more fully, understand Him better, feel more at home in His presence, find cause to praise Him more, and have a deeper relationship with Him.

Prayer Is the Key to Relationship

Intentional dialogue with God ultimately establishes and deepens our relationship with Him. The purpose of prayer is that we might know God better, experience more of His love, and have an abiding awareness of His work in our lives. Talking *to* God doesn't build relationship. Communicating *with* God does.

A relationship with God, of course, is very personal. In fact, it is the most intimate relationship you can ever know. Nobody knows you as God knows you. Nobody loves you as God loves you. Nobody desires good for your life more than God does. In prayer—in genuine communication with God—you will soon discover not only more about God, but more about yourself as God's beloved child. There is no more exciting or enriching experience!

Your individual relationship with God is unique. This is true for every relationship you have with another person, and it is no less true in your relationship with God. Your prayers must be *your* prayers. Your communication with God is *your* communication. While written or formalized prayers have their place in certain group settings, your times of communication with God should be marked by your own original speech. Prayer is talking with God as you would talk to your dearest friend, your most eager supporter, your most loving mentor.

Because prayer is intensely personal, there can be no universal formulas for prayer. This study does not devote itself to a series of procedures or offer a lockstep recipe for prayer. Rather, it deals with some general principles that are basic to any person's prayer life. The specifics of your prayer relationship with God are as distinctive as any other aspect of your life and your ability to communicate.

As we approach this study in prayer, I encourage you to open yourself to the grand possibility that God has something to say to you that you will delight in hearing. He is eager to spend time with you and to develop a deep, intimate relationship with you that is marked by great joy and well-being.

Ultimately, prayer is to be experienced, not studied. In study we simply learn how to better communicate with God—and to that end, how to have a better relationship with our Creator. It is an experience to be pursued and a relationship to be valued beyond all others

LESSON 1

PREPARING TO COMMUNICATE WITH GOD

This book is for Bible study. It is not a stand-alone manual. I hope you will refer to your Bible again and again, and that you will feel free to mark specific words, underline phrases, or write in the margins of your personal Bible.

Many good communication books are on the market today. The Bible, however, is God's foremost book about God's communication with us. It is the source from which we receive new insights and eternal wisdom. It is the reference book to which we must return continually to make certain that what we hear from other people is acceptable to God and, therefore, is true wisdom that we can apply to our daily lives. You should read and study the Bible on a daily basis. It will be far more valuable for you to write what you learn from this study guide into the margins and end pages of your Bible than for you to write passages of the Bible or insights you may have into this book.

Keys to Study

You will be asked in this guide to identify with the concepts and verses that are presented by answering one or more of these questions:

- What new insight have you gained?
- Have you ever had a similar experience?
- How do you feel about this?
- In what way are you challenged to act?

Insights

A spiritual insight is something that involves a new degree of understanding. It lies beyond a literal understanding of a fact or idea. For example, you may have read a particular passage in the Bible many times, and even studied it or meditated upon it diligently. You may think there is nothing more that you can learn from the passage. And then, God surprises you! Suddenly, He reveals new meaning to you. That is a spiritual insight.

Insights are usually very personal—most of them involve some way in which the passage has meaning to what you personally have experienced or are experiencing now. Spiritual insights are the direct work of the Holy Spirit in our lives. They are a part of His function as the Spirit of truth. It is the Spirit who reveals to us precisely what is important for us to know or learn at any given moment in our lives so that we might grow in Christ.

Ask the Holy Spirit to give you insights every time you open your Bible to read and study it. I believe that's one prayer that God delights in answering with a resounding *yes!* In fact, if you haven't gained new spiritual insights after reading several passages from God's Word, you probably haven't been engaged in the process of genuine study. The person who truly studies God's Word with an open heart and an eagerness to hear from the Holy Spirit is going to have spiritual insights on a regular basis.

As you receive spiritual insights, make notes about them. The benefit to you lies in the future. When you look back in the margins of your Bible and read what God has shown you or spoken to your heart in the past, and then reflect on how that insight has manifested in the subsequent months or years of your life, your faith will grow. I believe it is always a good idea to add a date to the spiritual-insight notes you make.

Experiences

Each of us comes to God's Word with a different background in reading and studying the Bible and with a different level of understanding about the Bible's content. Therefore, each individual has a slightly different perspective on the Scripture reading. In a group setting, these differences can sometimes create problems. For example, people with a long history of regularly reading God's Word may lose patience with those who are just beginning to read and study the Bible, and beginners may feel overwhelmed or lost.

What we do have in common are life experiences. We can point to times in which we have found the truth of a Bible passage to be highly relevant to our lives. We can recall times when the Bible confirmed, encouraged, convicted, challenged, or directed us in some way. We have experiences about which we can say, "I know that truth in the Bible is real because of what happened to me," or, "That passage speaks to me because it is directly related to an experience I am having."

Our experiences do not make the Bible true. The Bible is truth, period. It is as we share our experiences and how they relate to God's Word, however, that we discover how far-reaching and amazing the Bible really is. God's Word applies to human life in more ways than we ever thought! When we share our Bible-related experiences, we see how God's Word speaks to each person, to every aspect of human nature, and to every human condition or problem.

Sharing experiences is important for your spiritual growth. Not only do you benefit from hearing the experiences of others, but you benefit from sharing your own experiences. Although your prayer life is highly personal, I encourage you to share what prayer has meant to you in building your relationship with God so that you might encourage others. Conversely, although others may have a prayer life different from yours, I encourage you to be open to what you may be able to learn, adapt, and apply. I caution you to keep these discussions focused on the Scriptures, and not simply talk about prayer experiences for the sake of experience. I also advise you to use the Scriptures as your basis for evaluating any prayer experience that a person shares.

Our tendency in sharing experiences is to judge the experience of another person in the light of our own experience. A judgmental attitude—especially toward a person's very private and intimate experiences in prayer—not only can do great harm to the spiritual growth of another person, but also can cause great friction within a group. Listen. Discuss. Talk about what the Scriptures say and mean to you. But be very careful not to judge or to condemn others as they share with vulnerability the experiences they may have had in communicating with God.

Emotional Response

Just as we have unique life experiences, so we have our own emotional responses to God's Word. No emotional response is more valid than another. One person may be frightened by the message of a particular verse or passage. Another person may feel great joy or relief at reading the same words. Face your emotions honestly, and allow others the freedom to share their emotions fully. Every emotion is valid.

This is not to say that our emotions give validity to the Scriptures or that emotions can be trusted as a gauge of faith. Our faith is always to be based on what God says, not what we feel. The Scriptures are true regardless of the emotions they evoke in us. At the same time, we must recognize that the Bible does have an emotional impact on us. We cannot read the Bible with an open heart and mind and not have an emotional response to it.

Perhaps in no other field of study is this more true than in a study of prayer. Prayer involves the baring of our innermost being to God. It is an experience in which all emotions are likely to be felt and displayed. Some people allow themselves to be much more vulnerable emotionally than others. Their responses to particular Scripture passages about prayer may evoke tears or feelings of great elation, longing, or conviction. Allow for the expression of these emotions without judgment in your group setting. Recognize that God has created us with emotions and that the Scriptures do cause emotional response. As we identify how we feel about God's messages to us we often can begin to overcome any inertia that keeps us from actually applying God's Word to our lives. For example, if we are afraid of prayer, why is that so? If we feel great sorrow when we read God's Word or pray, why? Answering such questions can begin a healing process.

Bible study groups sometimes get sidetracked by opinions. This can lead quickly to debate, distrust, and confusion. Focus your group sharing on feelings and experiences, not opinions. Scholarly commentaries certainly have their place in teaching us the background of specific passages. But a person's knowledge and opinion actually have little impact on other people within the context of group Bible study. What God says to us individually and directly is what we find to be truly significant. And God often speaks to us in the language of the heart—the silent language of our intuition, our emotions, our innermost desires, and our unvoiced longings. When we share feelings with one another, we grow closer together. When we share only opinions, we rarely grow closer as a community or find unity of spirit in Christ Jesus.

Challenges

As we read the Bible, we often come to some passage or insight that seems to speak directly to us. Something challenges us to change an aspect of our lives, to gulp and say, "I need to do something about that."

We may feel a conviction about sin in our lives. We may feel a need to correct something in the way we think or the way we act toward others. We may feel a clear call to do something new—acquire a new habit or start a new form of ministry to others. In my life God never ceases to challenge me just beyond my ability so that I must always rely upon Him to work in me and through me. God is never content with the status quo—He always wants us to grow more like His Son, Jesus Christ. As I read the Scriptures and pray, or talk about the Scriptures with other people and pray with them, I often feel those challenges to grow and extend myself. I believe it is vitally important, therefore, for us to be aware of the ways in which God may be speaking to us through His Word to challenge us, stretch us, change us, or cause our faith to grow.

God's ultimate reason for us to know His Word is that we might share His Word with others—in both our actions and words. God not only expects us to know and believe His Word, He expects us to *do* His Word—to keep His commandments, to be His witnesses, to carry on His mission in the world (James 1:22).

Perhaps in no other Christian discipline is this more true than in prayer. God expects us not only to know about prayer, but to pray. He longs to meet us in prayer and to convey to us individually and privately what He desires for us to think, say, and do. Our agenda for each day and for all of life is to be the product of our prayer life. Our very identity is forged as we pray. My full expectation is that as you engage in this study, God will speak to you about His desires for your prayer life so that He might develop an even closer relationship with you. Be open to His wooing, His commanding, His challenges to you.

Personal or Group Study?

This book has been designed for group study. If you don't have somebody to talk to about your insights, experiences, emotions, and challenges, I encourage you to find somebody. Perhaps you can start a Bible study in your home, using this book as a focal point. Perhaps you can talk to your pastor about organizing Bible study groups in your church. There is much to be learned on your own. There is much more to be learned as you become part of a small group that desires to grow in the Lord.

If you are using this book for a personal study, I encourage you to find someone with whom you can share the fruit of what you learn and experience as a result. You may be able to share with a spouse, child, or close friend some of the insights you have into the Scripture or prayer.

You'll find personal benefit in giving voice to what you have learned. Make certain that your sharing, however, is not in the context of admonition, and that it doesn't degenerate into a debate.

Keep the Bible Central

A tendency of a group devoted to the study of prayer is for the group to become a prayer group rather than a Bible study group. Keep the Bible at the center of all you do.

Because prayer is intensely personal, and can be emotional, a second tendency of a study group on prayer is for the group to become a support or therapy group. Such groups have their time and place, but that is not the purpose of this study. I encourage you to gather around God's Word as if you were gathering around a banquet table for a spiritually nutritious meal. Remember, your time together should be spent in a *study* of the Scriptures.

Prayer

As you begin your Bible study, ask God to give you spiritual eyes to see what He wants you to see and spiritual ears to hear what He wants you to hear. Ask Him to give you new insights, to recall to your memory experiences that relate to what you read, and to help you identify clearly your emotional responses to His Word. Ask Him to reveal to you what He desires for you to be, say, and do.

As you conclude your time of study, ask the Lord to seal what you have learned in your heart so you will never forget it. Ask Him to transform you more into the likeness of Jesus Christ as you meditate on what you have studied. And above all, ask Him to give you the courage to become, say, and do what He has challenged you to become, say, and do.

As we discussed in the introduction, open yourself up as you pray—individually and as a group—to God's answers. Be keenly aware that He desires to have a dialogue with you about prayer. He desires to speak to your heart during and after your study time.

Consider these questions:

- *What new insights into prayer do you hope to gain from this study?*

  _____

  _____

- *In what areas have you struggled with prayer in the past? In what areas have you felt fulfillment in your prayer life? How have you been trained to pray?*

  _____

  _____

- *How do you feel about prayer?*

  _____

  _____

- *Are you open to being challenged to grow in your prayer life? Do you have a desire for deeper and richer communication with God?*

_____

_____

LESSON 2

GOD'S INVITATION TO PRAYER

Communication—or rather, failure to communicate—is a major problem in our world today. So often we don't say what we mean, we have difficulty putting our feelings into words, and we leave people with misunderstanding. Whether in the family, the workplace, or the church, we have problems communicating.

Many people also have problems communicating with God. They are uncomfortable talking to God, they wonder if He has heard what they have said, or they are confused or frustrated in their lack of ability to say what they mean.

The foremost problem in communication, however, is not any of the situations mentioned above. The foremost problem in both our human relationships and our relationship with God is a failure to *try* to communicate. If a person never opens his mouth and his heart to others, communication is stymied. Without an effort to *start* communicating, there can be no growth in one's ability to communicate.

The problem is not new. Repeatedly in the Bible, God invited His prophets to communicate with Him—He was seeking to open a dialogue, engage in a conversation, begin a discussion. God extends the same invitation to you and me today. He asks us to start the process with Him so He can build a relationship with us.

In Jeremiah 33:1–3 we find one of God's invitations to pray:

Moreover the word of the LORD came to Jeremiah a second time, while he was still shut up in the court of the prison, saying, "Thus says the LORD who made it, the LORD who formed it to establish it (the LORD is His name): 'Call to Me, and I will answer you, and show you great and mighty things, which you do not know.'"

At the time this word came to Jeremiah, he was in prison for disagreeing with the leaders of Jerusalem, who wanted to align themselves with the Egyptians to the south in order to defeat the Babylonians, who were invading Israel from the east. The Lord had told Jeremiah that His people would be taken into captivity by the Babylonians for seventy years. Jeremiah, therefore, had recommended to the leader in Jerusalem that they surrender peacefully and voluntarily—from his perspective, God's word was already coming to pass, so there was no point in fighting against it. The leaders responded by putting Jeremiah in prison.

"Call to Me"

There are three great messages in this word of the Lord to Jeremiah. First, God says, "Call to Me." There's probably no better place for a person to catch up on his or her prayer life than behind bars! Although we may not be behind physical bars or residing in a public prison, we very often are isolated through a series of events or problems so that we find ourselves feeling alone and captive to our circumstances. In those times our attention very often turns to God. Our cry is usually, "God, get me out of this place" or "God, get me out of this situation." Sometimes we may even attempt to barter with God, saying, in effect, "God, get me out of here so I can serve You better and read the Scripture and pray more than I have in the past."

In reality, however, the "prison" in which we find ourselves may be the very place that God has designated for us to learn better how to serve Him, read the Bible, and pray more. This is especially true when the prison is one of our own making—a prison marked by our sin or error, our emotional problems, our relationship problems with others, our self-created financial problems, or our self-inflicted health problems. Our healing lies not in our deliverance from the problem, but in developing a relationship with God in the midst of the problem.

God made no mention of Jeremiah's release from prison in this passage. He simply said, "Call to Me." God is far more interested in establishing a relationship with us and communicating with us within our situation than He is in changing our circumstances or releasing us from our problems. The lessons that we learn within life's problems are valuable for all eternity. They are greater than any lessons we might learn from a miraculous deliverance from our pain, suffering, or trouble.

God calls us to pray within the struggles of life. Prayer is the shortest distance between problems and solutions, difficulties and remedies, questions and answers. The distance between your knees and the floor is the shortest distance to seeing God at work in your life.

- *Have you had an experience in which you found yourself turning to God* within *a struggle or problem?*

_____

_____

- *What insight do you have into why we often do not make prayer our first resort in times of trouble?*

_____

_____

Always Available

God wants us to come to Him as His beloved daughter or son in order that He might be with us at any moment in our lives. He makes Himself immediately and personally available to us at any time of day or night, no matter what we are facing.

No person who has called out to God has ever heard a busy signal or a recorded message from an angelic being saying, "God is occupied right now. At the tone, please leave a message and He'll get back to you." God is *available*. He says, "Call to Me. I'm here."

We have the right to talk to God at any time, anywhere, and in the midst of any situation. His promise to us is this: "I will answer you."

What the Word Says	What the Word Says to Me
The LORD will hear when I call to Him. (Ps. 4:3)	------------------------------- -------------------------------
Call upon Me in the day of trouble; I will deliver you, and you shall glorify Me. (Ps. 50:15)	------------------------------- ------------------------------- -------------------------------

- *In what ways do you feel challenged in your prayer life?*

  _____

  _____

"I Will Answer You"

God encourages us to call on Him with the sure promise that He will hear and answer. We may not sense His presence, but He is always there.

People often fail us in their promises to be there for us. God does not fail us. There are times when we don't like God's answer to us, but He answers us nonetheless. He has three main answers to our petitions:

- Yes.
- No.
- Wait.

Each is an equally valid answer. We don't tend to see them as equally valid, however. The only answer we often accept from God is yes. I frequently hear people say, "Praise God, He answered my prayer! He said yes to what I requested." I have never heard a person say with exuberance, "Praise God! He said no to what I requested!"

We are self-centered people and we want God to give us what we desire. When God answers no, or wait, it is usually because we haven't fully waited upon the Lord to discover His will or direction for our lives. In such times these answers spare us heartache, keep us from error, or put us into a situation of growth so that we will be ready to receive the fullness of God's blessing in our lives.

A yes answer is not guaranteed solely because a person is living right. Sometimes a no is necessary because His answer to us affects another person who is not living right. What we can know with certainty is that God's answer is always for our protection and His motivation toward us is always love. He has our best interests at heart.

- *Have you ever asked something of God and received a yes answer? How did you feel?*

  _____

  _____

- *Have you ever asked something of God and received an answer of no? How did you feel?*

  _____

  _____

- *Have you ever asked something of God and received an answer of wait? How did you feel?*

  _____

  _____

- *In each of the above situations, what was your response? What was the outcome?*

  _____

  _____

I know people who, when they receive an answer from God that they do not like, turn immediately to their Bibles in hope of finding another answer they like better. Some read aloud a verse of Scripture with the hope that God will change His mind. They are trying to get God to rethink His decision. That never works. God's answer is God's answer. We are wise to accept it.

If the answer we receive is no, we are equally wise to ask God if His reason for denying our request has to do with sin in our lives. We can ask Him to reveal to us what is keeping us from being in a position to receive the yes answer we want. We can ask Him to evaluate the desires of our heart and show us which ones are not in keeping with His perfect plan for our lives. Likewise, if the answer we receive is wait, we are wise to be alert before God so when the time is right, we can act to receive what God has for us.

In both cases, we are submitting our lives to God, engaging in an ongoing process of communication with God, and opening ourselves up to a deeper relationship with Him. No and wait answers can be very productive for our spiritual growth, even though they are seldom the answers we want initially.

The fact is, we can't hurry God in His answers. We can't change His mind. He is more interested in our eternal future—our growth, our faith, our obedience, our character—than in making us happy in the current moment. God's answers are for our good, and He will not be swayed from giving us what is best for us. Only Jesus had all of His prayers answered with a yes. We simply do not have perfect wisdom and understanding.

Our response to God's no and wait answers is critical. If we respond with a submissive will, then we are serving and relating to the Lord out of love. If we rebel against Him, we have evidence that our relationship with Him and service to Him are bound by duty, not love. God's desire, of course, is that His relationship with us be characterized by spontaneous love and devotion, not stubborn or prideful duty.

What the Word Says	What the Word Says to Me
Give ear, O LORD, to my prayer; And attend to the voice of my supplications. In the day of my trouble I will call upon You, For You will answer me. (Ps. 86:6–7)	
He shall call upon Me, and I will answer him; I will be with him in trouble. . . .And show him My salvation. (Ps. 91:15–16)	

The LORD will answer and say to
His people,
"Behold, I will send you grain and
new wine and oil,
And you will be satisfied by them."
(Joel 2:19)

My soul, wait silently for God
alone,
For my expectation is from Him.
(Ps. 62:5)

- *In what ways are you feeling challenged in your prayer life?*

_____

_____

"Show You Great and Mighty Things"

When God invited Jeremiah to call to Him, He said, "I will answer you, and show you great and mighty things, which you do not know."

Many of our petitions to God involve other people and our decisions related to them. We often ask God to bless our family members and friends and to exercise judgment on our enemies. But then many of us go about our daily business without ever considering what it is that God might want *us* to do, or what He might want to teach us and show us. There are many instances in which we need to admit that we "do not know." It is only then that we will open ourselves to receive God's divine guidance and wisdom. Note the things God said He would show to Jeremiah:

Great things. God alone is truly great. There is nothing greater than seeing God with spiritual eyes, hearing Him with spiritual ears, and gaining an understanding of what He is able and willing to do. God alone knows our past deeds and our future potential. He is the Holy One, the great Creator, Sustainer, and Lover of humankind. God wanted to show *Himself* to Jeremiah. He wanted to reveal to Jeremiah what was possible for Jeremiah's future and the future of all God's people.

When we read the Scriptures, we see the greatness of God on virtually every page. When we look at the lives of great Christians through the ages, we see the greatness of God at work. When we reflect back over the experiences of our own lives, we have evidence of God's greatness. One of the foremost things that God desires to show you through your prayer relationship with Him is His own greatness. He wants to communicate to you His vast love and power and wisdom—all of which He makes available to you.

- *How do you feel about the fact that God desires to reveal Himself to you?*

Mighty things. God also promised to reveal to Jeremiah "mighty things, which you do not know." The word *mighty* in our current English usage does not mean what it meant at the time the Bible was written. The term usually is used to refer to great fortified cities, ones that were walled in. The word is a reference to things that are hidden, secret, and therefore, secure.

God desires to reveal to us the things that are inaccessible to us through any other means outside of prayer. It is through our communication with God that He reveals to us the secret treasures of understanding and discernment that are "hidden" in the Scriptures. It is through our conversations with God that He reveals to us the as-yet-unknown answers to our questions and the solutions to our problems. When we come to the Lord with a pure and humble heart, seeking above all an intimate relationship with Him, then God can trust us with the precious riches of His power.

I have gone to God repeatedly through the years of my ministry to ask Him for specific guidance and direction on a wide range of matters. Not once has He failed to answer. Many times His answer has involved things that had been hidden to me. God has led me to ask questions I would not otherwise have asked, to seek information I would not otherwise have sought, to probe issues I would not otherwise have touched, or to contact people I would not otherwise have called. In the process of my obeying God's guidance,

He has given me access to resources and ideas and solutions that were previously unknown to me. In every instance, what God revealed to me was for my ultimate and eternal good. I have no doubt whatsoever that what He has done for me, He will do for you.

God's revelation of mighty things may not come immediately, or even quickly. In some cases, we may not yet be able to receive the information or make full use of the resources that are revealed to us. But God will not keep from us anything we need to know. He responds to our cries for help not only by revealing Himself as the source of all our help, but also by supplying all the resources that we need.

- *How do you feel about the fact that God desires to reveal answers and solutions to you as you develop a relationship with Him in prayer?*

_____

_____

There are some things that God alone knows—things that will never be revealed to any person. Furthermore, with our finite minds, none of us can ever fully comprehend or encompass God's wisdom, power, and love. What we can know are the things that we need to know in order to keep God's commandments and follow His will for our lives. What God tells us to do, He will equip us to do—including the equipment of adequate knowledge, courage, patience, fortitude, wisdom, discernment, resources, and compassion.

What the Word Says	What the Word Says to Me
The secret things belong to the LORD our God, but those things which are revealed belong to us and to our children forever, that we may do all the words of this law. (Deut. 29:29) Yours, O LORD, is the greatness, The power and the glory, The victory and the majesty; For all that is in heaven and in earth is Yours;	_____ _____ _____ _____ _____ _____ _____ _____ _____ _____

Yours is the kingdom, O LORD,
And You are exalted as head over
all.
Both riches and honor come from
You,
And You reign over all.
In Your hand is power and might;
In Your hand it is to make great
And to give strength to all.
Now therefore, our God,
We thank You
And praise Your glorious name.
 (1 Chron. 29:11–13)

Every valley shall be exalted
And every mountain and hill
brought low;
The crooked places shall be made
straight
And the rough places smooth;
The glory of the LORD shall be
revealed. (Isa. 40:4–5a)

You are great in counsel and
mighty in work, for your eyes are
open to all the ways of the sons of
men, to give everyone according to
his ways and according to the fruit
of his doings. (Jer. 32:19)

The LORD will answer and say to
His people,
"Behold, I will send you grain and
new wine and oil,
And you will be satisfied by them."
(Joel 2:19)

My soul, wait silently for God
alone,
For my expectation is from Him.
(Ps. 62:5)

- *In what ways are you feeling challenged in your prayer life?*

_____

_____

The Invitation to Knock, Ask, Seek

Jesus reissued the invitation of God to "call to Me" in Matthew 7:7, which is part of the Sermon on the Mount: "Ask, and it will be given to you; seek, and you will find; knock, and it will be opened to you." The promise of Jesus to His followers is just as sure as that of God to Jeremiah: the one who asks, seeks, and knocks, will receive God's answer and supply. Asking, seeking, and knocking are aspects of our prayer life.

Ask. We are to ask for the things we need. Some people seem reluctant to pray for the material goods and resources they need, but God invites us to do so. In fact, He tells us that we often don't have what we need because we haven't asked (James 4:2).

Seek. We are to seek understanding and knowledge so we can develop relationships with others. The goal of seeking is to find someone, and our primary goal is to seek God. We may need a certain amount of knowledge and understanding to come into relationship with the right people at the right time, but part of God's promise to us is that He will help us find what and whom we desire to find.

Knock. We are to knock on the doors of opportunity that appear before us, responding with our faith to the potential for good that God places in our path. God desires for us to fulfill the potential He has placed in us. He wants us to feel satisfaction and fulfillment in what we do for Him, in Him, and through Him.

The basis for all answered prayer is God's love. He responds to our petitions for things, relationships, and fulfillment because He loves us. Our asking, seeking, and knocking are all to be done within the context of our ongoing daily communication with God. Our needs change daily. New opportunities come our way on a daily basis. Relationships are built day by day. Therefore, our communication with God must be daily. Jesus referred to a daily intimate relationship with God as "abiding" in God. The communication of a person who is abiding is frequent, without barriers, and deeply personal and meaningful. As we develop that kind of communication with God, we truly are in a position for Him to reveal to us and to provide for us all that we can possibly desire, in part because our desires will be His desires for us.

What the Word Says	What the Word Says to Me
For everyone who asks receives, and he who seeks finds, and to him who knocks it will be opened. Or what man is there among you who, if his son asks for bread, will give him a stone? Or if he asks for a fish, will he give him a serpent? If you then, being evil, know how to give good gifts to your children, how much more will your Father who is in heaven give good things to those who ask Him! (Matt. 7:8–11)	_____ _____ _____ _____ _____ _____ _____ _____ _____ _____ _____ _____
If you abide in Me, and My words abide in you, you will ask what you desire, and it shall be done for you. By this My Father is glorified, that you bear much fruit; so you will be My disciples. (John 15:7–8)	_____ _____ _____ _____ _____ _____

- *What new insights do you have into God's invitation to you to pray— to communicate with Him and grow in your relationship with Him?*

_____

_____

- *In what ways are you feeling a renewed call to pray?*

_____

_____

LESSON 3

PRAYING WITH AUTHORITY

The prophet Elijah and King Ahab had been in conflict for some time over idolatry and false worship in Israel before Elijah declared a showdown. Elijah commanded the king to call the Israelites to Mount Carmel, as well as the prophets of Baal and Asherah who were supported strongly by Queen Jezebel. When all parties were assembled, Elijah said to the people, "How long will you falter between two opinions? If the LORD is God, follow Him; but if Baal, follow him" (1 Kings 18:21). The people didn't respond, so Elijah challenged the prophets to a duel of sorts.

The prophets of Baal and the prophet Elijah were each given a bull to sacrifice. Elijah said, "You call on the name of your gods, and I will call on the name of the LORD; and the God who answers by fire, He is God" (1 Kings 18:24). The prophets of Baal agreed to this plan and they spent all day—from morning until the time of the evening sacrifice—crying out to Baal, leaping about the altar, and cutting themselves with knives, all without any result whatsoever.

Meanwhile, Elijah took twelve stones to make an altar to the Lord, surrounded the altar with a trench, and then cut wood and soaked both it and the sacrificial bull with water until the trench was also filled with water—in fact, he soaked the wood and sacrifice with water three times. At the time of the evening sacrifice, Elijah prayed:

LORD God of Abraham, Isaac, and Israel, let it be known this day that You are God in Israel and I am Your servant, and that I have done all these things at Your word. Hear me, O LORD, hear me, that this people may know that You are the LORD God, and that You have turned their hearts back to You again. (1 Kings 18:36–37)

When Elijah had finished his prayer, the fire of the Lord fell and consumed the sacrifice, as well as the wood, the stones, the dust, and all the water in the trench. When the people saw what had happened, they fell on their faces and said, "The LORD, He is God! The LORD, He is God!" (v. 39).

What a wonderful example of praying with boldness and authority! Elijah didn't pray in secret, off in some corner where nobody could see or hear him. He prayed openly and publicly. There was nothing tricky or shady about what he did; there was no doubt about what he said.

God has filled the Scriptures with promises. Oh, how few of them we claim as our own! A man once said to me, "I feel that when I come into the throne room of God, I just tiptoe around. I'm afraid of what God may say or do." I believe his behavior is that of many Christians.

God, however, tells us to come boldly into His presence. He grants us the privilege to come before Him with authority because of our position in Christ Jesus. We are to be bold in believing with our faith that God is going to do what He desires to do and what He says He will do in our lives.

What the Word Says

For we do not have a High Priest who cannot sympathize with our weaknesses, but was in all points tempted as we are, yet without sin. Let us therefore come boldly to the throne of grace, that we may obtain mercy and find grace to help in time of need. (Heb. 4:15–16)

Therefore, brethren, having

What the Word Says to Me

----

boldness to enter the Holiest by
the blood of Jesus ... let us draw
near with a true heart in full assurance of faith. (Heb. 10:19, 22)

_____
_____
_____
_____

- *How do you feel when you enter God's throne room?*

_____

_____

- *In what ways do you feel challenged by these verses from Hebrews?*

_____

_____

What Is Our Authority?

In 2 Chronicles 20, we read about a great multitude of people who rose up against King Jehoshaphat and the people of Israel. Three groups of people—the Moabites, the Ammonites, and the people of Mount Seir—launched a major assault against Jerusalem.

Jehoshaphat was afraid, but rather than cower in fear, verse 3 says he "set himself to seek the LORD." He proclaimed a fast throughout all Judah and called the people together to join him in seeking the Lord. He stood before the people in the house of the Lord and prayed, "O LORD God of our fathers, are You not God in heaven, and do You not rule over all the kingdoms of the nations, and in Your hand is there not power and might, so that no one is able to withstand You?" (v. 6).

Jehoshaphat was not doubting the power of God. Rather, he was affirming his belief in God. He was declaring that he was putting all of his trust in the God of unlimited power. He went on to pray:

> *Are You not our God, who drove out the inhabitants of this land before Your people Israel, and gave it to the descendants of Abraham Your friend forever? And they dwell in it, and have built You a sanctuary in it for Your name, saying, "If disaster comes upon us—sword, judgment, pestilence, or famine—we will stand before this temple and in Your presence (for Your name is in this temple),*

and cry out to You in our affliction, and You will hear and save."
And now, here are the people of Ammon, Moab, and Mount Seir—
whom You would not let Israel invade when they came out of the
land of Egypt, but they turned from them and did not destroy them—
here they are, rewarding us by coming to throw us out of Your pos-
session which You have given us to inherit. O our God, will You
not judge them? For we have no power against this great multitude
that is coming against us; nor do we know what to do, but our eyes
are upon You. (vv. 7–12)

Jehoshaphat stated very plainly that he, even as king of the land, was standing in a position of total humility and weakness before the Lord. He claimed no authority in or for himself. He said to the Lord:

- You are the One who gave us this land.
- You are the One who has allowed Your people to dwell in it and build a sanctuary for You in it.
- You are the One who said that we should cry out to You in our affliction and You would hear and save us.
- You are the One who told us to spare these enemy people when we first came to occupy this land.
- You are the only One capable of judging these enemies who are rising against us—we have no power and no plan.

He concluded by saying, "Our eyes are squarely on You and on no other." In sum, Jehoshaphat was saying, "If You don't exercise Your authority in this matter, we are doomed. We are putting our entire trust and confidence in You and You alone."

There is no trace of egotism in Jehoshaphat. He made no demand that God do something that God did not desire to do. Jehoshaphat claimed no authority in himself, and also no power for himself.

- *Have you had an experience in your life in which you knew with cer-*
  tainty that you had no power or authority apart from God?

_____

_____

- *What new insights do you have into the prayers of Elijah and Jehoshaphat?*

_____

_____

Authority vs. Power

Matthew 28:18 records the Great Commission that Jesus gave to His disciples. Jesus said,

> *All authority has been given to Me in heaven and on earth. Go therefore and make disciples of all the nations, baptizing them in the name of the Father and of the Son and of the Holy Spirit, teaching them to observe all things that I have commanded you; and lo, I am with you always, even to the end of the age.*

The word *power* refers to the ability to bring about, execute, or act with hindrances removed. This word refers to a divine capacity, a divine right or privilege. Jesus declared that He has the authority to send out His own disciples.

In Acts 1:8, the word *power* is translated from the Greek word *dunamis*.

> *But you shall receive power [dunamis] when the Holy Spirit has come upon you; and you shall be witnesses to Me in Jerusalem, and in all Judea and Samaria, and to the end of the earth.*

This word for power refers to the *dynamic ability* that will be given to the disciples so that they can be witnesses. This is an enabling, life-changing, highly effective power.

Jesus was not turning over the fullness of His authority to His disciples—He retains His authority as Savior and Lord always. What He was imparting to His disciples through the Holy Spirit was the ability to do *whatever Jesus authorized them to do*. In other words, in their receiving the Holy Spirit, His disciples would receive the power to carry out the mission that Jesus was sending them on. Jesus is the

One who *possesses the authority* and *imparts the ability* through the Holy Spirit.

This is a critical distinction for us to make. As Christians we do not have authority in and of ourselves. All authority resides in Christ Jesus, our Savior and Lord. But, we have been given power to carry out the commandments of Jesus on earth. Furthermore, we do not have this power in ourselves apart from the Holy Spirit. It is a power that is given to us by Jesus, and which we must actively receive from the Spirit.

Both words, *authority* and *power*, are recorded in Luke 9:1:

> *Then He called His twelve disciples together and gave them power and authority over all demons, and to cure diseases.*

Jesus sent out His twelve disciples to preach the kingdom of God and He gave them both power and authority for a ministry of healing and deliverance. He imparted to them the capacity for this type of ministry, as well as the power to do this ministry. In other words, He gifted them with both the *can-do* authority and *will-succeed* power.

Jesus expected His disciples to fulfill their mission because they had been fully equipped to do so. The same holds true for us. When God sends us out on a mission, He gives us both the ability to do the mission and the power that will ensure the mission is accomplished. He gives us everything we need.

Our Authority and Power in Prayer

God has called us to pray and has given every person the capacity to pray. Prayer is both a commandment of God and a mission. God has fully authorized us to pray and He has given us the privilege to call upon His name at any place and at any time. God can be accessed from anywhere on earth, at any moment in history. He has given us the name of Jesus—the greatest name on earth and in heaven—as our authority in which to pray.

Not only does God give us the authority to pray, but He empowers us to pray. He moves in us and through us by the Holy Spirit so that our prayers are effective. The believer who prays in Atlanta can be effective in bringing about spiritual change in Tehran. The believer who prays in southern California can be effective in bringing about God's blessing on the church in China. There is no distance in prayer. Prayer can affect any situation, alter any circumstance, and bring about any type of change anywhere on earth.

The questions are, Will we pray with boldness? Will we move forward in our faith, claiming all of the promises that God has given us in the Scriptures, knowing with full assurance that Jesus Christ is our authority and the Holy Spirit is our empowerment? Will we pray and believe and see God act?

Nothing other than prayer allows us as individual believers and collective groups of believers any greater potential to affect the state of an individual sinful heart and the state of world affairs. Think about it! Prayer is the most potent, effective, life-changing force given by God to humankind.

It is up to us, therefore, to pray. And to pray boldly and with the full force of our faith in Christ Jesus.

What the Word Says	What the Word Says to Me
Assuredly, I say to you, if you have faith and do not doubt, you will not only do what was done to the fig tree, but also if you say to this mountain, "Be removed and be cast into the sea," it will be done. And whatever things you ask in prayer, believing, you will receive. (Matt. 21:21–22)	....
You do not have because you do not ask. (James 4:2)	....
We have confidence toward God. And whatever we ask we receive from Him, because we keep His commandments and do those things that are pleasing in His sight. (1 John 3:21–22)	....

- *In what ways are you feeling challenged in your prayer life?*

_____

_____

Our Offense Against the Enemy of Our Souls

When we begin to pray with power, the enemy of our souls will come to us and say, "Why do you think you have the right to pray for that? Who do you think you are?"

Paul addressed this matter in Ephesians 6. He told the Ephesians that they must adopt a posture of boldness in prayer: "Be strong in the Lord and in the power of His might" (v. 10). Paul stated up front that our authority and power are clearly resident in and imparted by Christ Jesus. We are not bold or powerful in our own right.

He then reminded the Ephesians that the ever-present enemy is Satan. We are in mortal conflict with the devil and his demons. We battle against the wiles of the devil and wrestle against principalities, powers, rulers of the darkness of this age, and spiritual hosts of wickedness (vv. 11–12).

Anytime we begin to pray we can expect Satan to put up a fight against our prayers. How do we overcome him? Paul said we are to "take up the whole armor of God, that you may be able to withstand in the evil day, and having done all, to stand" (v. 13). Paul described this armor as

- the breastplate of righteousness;
- feet shod with the preparation of the gospel of peace
- the shield of faith, by which we are able to quench all the fiery darts of the enemy;
- the helmet of salvation;
- the sword of the Spirit, which is the word of God (vv. 14–17).

When we put on the whole armor of God, we are putting on the identity of Christ Jesus. We are recognizing that Christ alone is our authority. Jesus is our righteousness. He is our peace. He is the Author and Finisher of our faith. He is our Savior and the One who, by the power of the Holy Spirit, reminds us of the word of God and teaches us the deep meanings of God's Word. He has the full capacity to defeat the enemy at every turn, and He has imparted to us the capacity to defeat the enemy at specific times and places through our prayers.

Paul closed this illustration by telling the Ephesians that they were to pray always "with all prayer and supplication in the Spirit, being watchful to this end with all perseverance and supplication for all the saints" (v. 18).

Prayer is our offense against the devil's attacks and against his strongholds. Paul stated very clearly that we have the power of the Holy Spirit working in us and through us to make certain that we are able to exercise the authority of Christ successfully. Paul declared this to be a winning posture. We will not fail against the devil if we recognize the real enemy, put on the armor of Christ Jesus and take on the authority He alone imparts to us, and then pray with persevering, enduring faith.

None of us have either the authority or the power to stand against the devil on the basis of our own personality, intellect, or gifts. But in Christ, we have His authority and His power to soundly defeat the enemy regardless of what he may launch against us.

What a contrast this is to simply wishing and hoping in prayer that God will act. We must understand that God wants bold, assertive action in prayer. He wants us to pray as if we are fighting and defeating the most real of all enemies, not only in our personal lives but also on behalf of other believers.

- *What new insights do you have in your study of Ephesians 6:10–18?*

- *In your past experiences with prayer, have you ever felt weak in your battle against the devil? Have you felt strong? What made the difference?*

Praying with Perseverance

Paul admonished the Ephesians to pray "always ... being watchful to this end with all perseverance" (Eph. 6:18). Jesus repeatedly told His disciples to "watch and pray." Knowing we have the authority in Christ and the power to pray successfully means very little if we do not pray. Our command from God is to pray and to do so boldly and consistently, relying totally upon Him and exercising the full authority and power given to us by Jesus.

- *What new insights do you have into God's call to prayer?*

  _____

- *In what ways are you feeling challenged in your prayer life?*

  _____

LESSON 4

PRAYER AND FASTING

Our motivation in the Christian walk is always to be love—love for God and for others. Our behavior, and especially our acts of Christian piety must never be rooted in self-pride or displayed so that we draw attention to ourselves. In His Sermon on the Mount, Jesus made this very clear regarding three special areas of Christian behavior: almsgiving, prayer, and fasting. He said specifically about prayer and fasting,

> *When you pray, you shall not be like the hypocrites. For they love to pray standing in the synagogues and on the corners of the streets, that they may be seen by men. Assuredly, I say to you, they have their reward. But you, when you pray, go into your room, and when you have shut your door, pray to your Father who is in the secret place; and your Father who sees in secret will reward you openly. And when you pray, do not use vain repetitions as the heathen do. For they think that they will be heard for their many words. Therefore do not be like them. For your Father knows the things you have need of before you ask Him. . . . Moreover, when you fast, do not be like the hypocrites, with a sad countenance. For they disfigure their faces that they may appear to men to be fasting. Assuredly, I say to you, they have their reward. But you, when you fast, anoint your head and wash your face, so that you do not appear to men to be fasting, but to your Father who is in the secret place; and your Father who sees in secret will reward you openly. (Matt. 6:5–8, 16–18)*

In the last lesson, we discussed two examples of prayer—Elijah's prayer before the Israelites and the prophets of Baal and Asherah, and Jehoshaphat's prayer before the people of Israel. In these two examples, leaders openly expressed their faith and trust in God alone. They are bold examples of giving public witness through prayer. And a bold witness through prayer can only be made if it is the outgrowth of countless hours of private and personal prayer.

God desires to know us best. He is a jealous God who insists on being the foremost object of our affection and loyalty. When we pray, we are invited to disclose our innermost thoughts, feelings, and desires. The aspects of our deep inner spiritual life are best expressed to God alone. Sharing our secrets and desires with God results in a relationship with God, and as we share we open ourselves up to His healing, guiding, and comforting power and presence.

In contrast, public displays of prayer performed primarily to draw attention to oneself do nothing to further a relationship with God. The same is true for public displays of fasting. Such open displays of prayer and fasting bring attention solely to the person, they do not bring glory to God. The purpose of prayer and fasting is not that others might applaud the current spiritual state of a person, but that the person who is praying and fasting might be changed.

- *Have you ever been present when someone else made an open show of prayer and fasting? How did you feel?*

- *What new insights do you have into Jesus' teaching about prayer and fasting (Matt. 6:5–8, 16–18)?*

The Bible has repeated references to the "secret" nature of our relationship with God. This does not mean that we are to deny our relationship with God or keep our witness for Christ under wraps. Rather, it means that our relationship with God is to be first and foremost an intimate, warm, close, shut-away relationship with Him. It is intensely personal and private. When we have a deep relationship with the Lord, we can then speak and act publicly as He directs.

What the Word Says	What the Word Says to Me
He who dwells in the secret place of the Most High Shall abide under the shadow of the Almighty. (Ps. 91:1)	
Oh, how great is Your goodness, Which You have laid up for those who fear You, Which You have prepared for those who trust in You In the presence of the sons of men! You shall hide them in the secret place of Your presence From the plots of man; You shall keep them secretly in a pavilion From the strife of tongues. (Ps. 31:19–20)	
He reveals deep and secret things; He knows what is in the darkness, And light dwells with Him. (Dan. 2:22)	
O my dove, in the clefts of the rock, In the secret places of the cliff, Let me see your face, Let me hear your voice; For your voice is sweet, And your face is lovely. (Song 2:14)	

• *In what ways are you being challenged in your prayer life?*

_____

_____

The Purpose of Prayer and Fasting

Prayer and fasting are two of the foremost weapons we have in our battle against the enemy of our souls, the devil. The Word of God, our faith, praise, the name of Jesus, and the blood of Jesus are all weapons in our spiritual warfare against evil. Prayer and fasting are not just good things to do for our own spiritual growth and development; they are genuine spiritual weapons, mighty for battle. We must always be on guard that we are using these weapons correctly.

1. We must not use prayer and fasting to avoid doing the will of God. Some people turn to prayer and fasting as a substitute for obedient action. They think they can convince themselves and God that they are being obedient by praying and fasting about a situation, when in reality, they are avoiding the business that God has called them to do.

2. We must not think that prayer and fasting are a substitute for repenting of sin. Some people think that they can continue to sin in various areas of their lives if they balance that sin with a proper amount of prayer and fasting. No amount of prayer and fasting can atone for sin. The shed blood of Jesus Christ is the only atonement for sin. Prayer and fasting might strengthen your ability to turn away from sin and not give in to temptation, but they are not an antidote or a compensation for sin.

• *In your past experiences with fasting and prayer, what motivated you to fast and pray? How did you feel about fasting and prayer?*

_____

_____

The Proper Use of Prayer and Fasting

The real purpose for fasting is to bring the body and soul into subjection so that in prayer, a person is focused solely on God and His plans and purposes for that person's life.

Each of us has natural desires and appetites that are a part of our creation. These are to be satisfied in proper ways according to God's commandments so that the fulfillment of our desires and appetites brings about good to our bodies and souls. For example, we have an appetite for food, which is to be exercised within the boundaries of good nutrition and moderation. We have a desire for beauty, which is to be satisfied in purity. We have an appetite for sex, which is to be satisfied within the bounds of a marriage covenant. We have an appetite for sleep, which is to be met for the purposes of rejuvenation, not as an escape from life's responsibilities.

There are times, however, when God asks us to set aside these natural desires and appetites and concentrate solely on the spiritual dimension of our being. True fasting goes beyond skipping a meal or denying ourselves food for a period of time. It is a turning away from and a willful denying of all natural human desires and appetites so we might concentrate solely on the Lord and what He wants to say to us or accomplish in our lives.

God calls us to a time of fasting and prayer for many reasons:

- He may want to reveal to us an area of our lives that needs to be changed.
- He may want to express to us His desires, perhaps even a new direction or challenge He wants us to undertake.
- He may want us to intercede for others.

The ultimate purpose for fasting and prayer rests with God. When we fast, submitting all of our normal life patterns to Him, He has our full attention, and He can mold us completely and totally for His purposes. When we are in this spiritual state—completely yielded and submitted, totally humble before Him and reliant upon Him—God can guide our prayers like arrows to accomplish His will. He then can do the real transforming work in our inner spirit that causes us to speak and act more like Jesus Christ.

The Call to Fasting and Prayer

How does God call us to fasting and prayer? By giving us a *desire* to fast and pray. He may call to our minds a specific need or situation that we know requires an intense focus of prayer. Or He may simply place in our hearts a deep longing to be with Him. When God calls a person to fast and pray, that person will have a greater desire to pray and be with the Lord than to eat, sleep, or do any other activity.

A person may begin a period of fasting and prayer with a specific intent or purpose in mind. As the person begins to fast and pray, however, God often reveals a deeper purpose. God guides the prayer. God reveals His will. In the process, the person is changed and the things about which the person is praying are accomplished in the spirit realm.

Ultimately, God calls us to fast and pray so that we become more like Christ in our nature and more effective witnesses to His life-changing power. He calls us to fasting and prayer so that we can be changed and our prayers might truly defeat the devil.

What the Word Says	What the Word Says to Me
Till we all come to the unity of the faith and of the knowledge of the Son of God, to a perfect man, to the measure of the stature of the fullness of Christ; that we should no longer be children, tossed to and fro and carried about with every wind of doctrine, by the trickery of men, in the cunning craftiness of deceitful plotting, but, speaking the truth in love, may grow up in all things into Him who is the head—Christ. (Eph. 4:13–15)	----------------------------- ----------------------------- ----------------------------- ----------------------------- ----------------------------- ----------------------------- ----------------------------- ----------------------------- ----------------------------- ----------------------------- ----------------------------- -----------------------------
The effective, fervent prayer of a righteous man avails much. (James 5:16)	----------------------------- ----------------------------- -----------------------------

Benefits from Fasting and Prayer

God's call to fasting and prayer is always for our benefit. The Scriptures point out at least seven benefits of fasting and prayer.

1. Our attitudes, feelings, and thoughts are sifted, pruned, and purified so that God might entrust us with a greater ministry. By fasting and praying, we become more disciplined toward the things of the Father. We yield ourselves fully to Him. We give Him opportunity to cut away from us those things that will slow us down, do us in, or keep us from the plans and purposes He has designed for our lives.

Jesus fasted and prayed for forty days in the wilderness, and the end result was that He was perfected for ministry (Matt. 4:1–2, 11). Queen Esther fasted and prayed for three days, and the end result was that she was stripped of the fear that kept her from telling the king about the evil plot against her life and the lives of her people. (See Est. 4:15–16.)

Sometimes we feel unsettled or uneasy, but we can't pinpoint the reasons why. Fasting intensifies our focus on God, stripping away everything but Him, so He can show us not only what we are feeling and thinking, but what we need to change in our lives.

As we confront the devil in the areas of our lives that need change or refinement—using the Word of God as our foremost weapon as Jesus did in the wilderness—we are made stronger. We know that we have had a showdown with the enemy. We know the power of God's Word to defeat the enemy. We know that God is preparing us for His purposes.

2. We are able to discern more clearly the will of God for our lives in any given situation. Fasting clears our spiritual eyes and ears so we can accurately discern what God desires to reveal to us. If you are facing a major decision in your life, I strongly encourage you to go away for three days of fasting and prayer. Spend your time in the Word of God. Rein in your attention so you are totally focused on the things of God. Listen intently to what God desires to say to you. I feel confident He will reveal to you precisely what you are to do.

Daniel knew this to be true in his life. At a time when Daniel was greatly troubled over the sin of Israel, he set his face toward the Lord God "to make request by prayer and supplications, with fasting, sackcloth, and ashes" (Dan. 9:3). While he was praying and confessing his sin and the sin of Israel, the angel Gabriel came to him. Daniel wrote, "He informed me, and talked with me, and said,

'O Daniel, I have now come forth to give you skill to understand'" (Dan. 9:22).

Now God may not send you an angel to tell you what His will is for your life. In fact, it is very unlikely that He will do so. But God will give you understanding. You will begin to see in God's Word the answer to your question, the solution to your problem. He will speak to your innermost spirit by the Holy Spirit concerning what action you are to take. God is faithful to reveal all that you need to know so you can perform His will.

3. We are confronted with our sins and shortcomings so we might confess them to God, receive forgiveness for them, and walk in greater righteousness. There may be an area in your life—perhaps a habit or a persistent attitude—that you just can't seem to change. Many times these habits are broken as we fast and pray.

At other times, the Lord reveals to us something in our lives that we need to confront and correct. We may not have been aware of it before. But as the Lord reveals it to us, we can respond immediately, "Lord, please forgive me of this and change me so I will not behave or think this way in the future."

Fasting and prayer cleanse us and purify us as we face the temptations of Satan that have kept us entangled in sin and error.

4. We experience a release of supernatural power in our lives. The outcome of genuine fasting and prayer is spiritual growth, including a renewed outpouring of supernatural power.

The disciples of Jesus prayed for a child who was demon-possessed, but they saw no results. Jesus rebuked the demon and it left the boy. The disciples later asked why they had been ineffective. Jesus answered, "This kind does not go out except by prayer and fasting" (Matt. 17:21). Certain problems and situations cannot be resolved apart from fasting and prayer—and the subsequent release of supernatural power against a stronghold that has been erected by the enemy (2 Cor. 10:4).

As Paul and Barnabas traveled in ministry, they made many disciples in Lystra, Iconium, and Antioch. They exhorted the disciples to continue in the faith, appointed elders in every church, "prayed with fasting," and "commended them to the Lord in whom they had believed" (Acts 14:22–23). What was the purpose of prayer and fasting? To release increased supernatural power into the lives of these believers so they might remain true to the Lord and endure any kind of tribulation that came against them.

This is an important reason for us to practice prayer and fasting—that we might be strengthened against the temptations of the enemy and have the power of the Holy Spirit manifested in and through our lives so we can endure any persecution or trouble that comes our way.

5. *We can make an effect on national issues and concerns through our prayers.* We have already noted how Jehoshaphat called the people to fasting and prayer. At the conclusion of Jehoshaphat's prayer, the Lord spoke through a prophet with the precise plan they were to follow. The battle plan was amazing—send out the choir before the soldiers! (See 2 Chron. 20:18–23.) But the plan worked, and it brought all the glory to God.

As we fast and pray for our nation, God will move. He will pour out His Spirit, in His ways and in His timing. We can count on it.

6. *We can help build up God's people.* Prayer is the generator of the church. It gives power to its ministers—pastors, teachers, evangelists, and those who engage in very practical ministries of helping others in need. It propels outreach to the lost. It creates a climate in which evangelistic efforts succeed.

When Nehemiah heard about the plight of his people and the destruction of the walls of Jerusalem, he "sat down and wept, and mourned for many days; [he] was fasting and praying before the God of heaven" (Neh. 1:4). As we hear of believers who are being persecuted in other nations, of believers who are falling into sin, of believers who are becoming lukewarm in the faith, we need to fast and pray that God will rebuild and renew and strengthen His people to withstand the enemy and endure his assault. God will hear and answer our prayers.

7. *Our minds are sharpened.* When we fast and pray our minds are quickened so that we understand the Scriptures as never before. We are sensitive to God's timing and direction with an increased awareness and ability to discern. We are keenly aware of what God desires to do and accomplish not only in our lives, but in the lives of others around us. When we fast and pray, the pollutants that have clogged

our ability to perceive and to think and to feel are removed so that
we can move freely in the flow of God's Holy Spirit.

What the Word Says	What the Word Says to Me
Then Jesus was led up by the Spirit into the wilderness to be tempted by the devil. And when He had fasted forty days and forty nights. . . . the devil left Him, and behold, angels came and ministered to Him. (Matt. 4:1–2, 11)	_____
There is a God in heaven who reveals secrets. (Dan. 2:28)	_____
For the weapons of our warfare are not carnal but mighty in God for pulling down strongholds, casting down arguments and every high thing that exalts itself against the knowledge of God, bringing every thought into captivity to the obedience of Christ. (2 Cor. 10:4–5)	_____
Seek the LORD while He may be found, Call upon Him while He is near. Let the wicked forsake his way, And the unrighteous man his thoughts; Let him return to the LORD, And He will have mercy on him; And to our God, For He will abundantly pardon. "For My thoughts are not your thoughts, Nor are your ways My ways," says the LORD. "For as the heavens are higher than the earth,	_____

So are My ways higher than your
ways,
And My thoughts than your
thoughts." (Isa. 55:6–9)

When I wept and chastened my
soul with fasting,
That became my reproach. . . .
But as for me, my prayer is to You,
O LORD, in the acceptable time;
O God, in the multitude of Your
mercy,
Hear me in the truth of Your
salvation.
Deliver me out of the mire,
And let me not sink;
Let me be delivered from those
who hate me,
And out of the deep waters. (Ps.
69:10, 13–14)

- *In what ways are you feeling challenged to fast and pray?*

_____

_____

Follow Up with Action

Fasting and prayer are to be followed up with action. Esther had to confront Haman in the presence of the king. After fasting and praying, Cornelius took the message of the gospel to the Gentiles (Acts 10:30). The result of Paul's fasting was increased missionary service. (See 2 Cor. 6:5 and 11:27.)

God very clearly called His people to action in Isaiah 58. The people asked God, "Why have we fasted . . . and You have not seen?" The Lord responded to them, "In fact, in the day of your fast you find pleasure, And exploit all your laborers. Indeed you fast for strife and debate, And to strike with the fist of wickedness" (vv. 3–4). God pointed out that their motives were wrong and that they were using fasting as a substitute for right action. He said,

Is this not the fast that I have chosen:
To loose the bonds of wickedness,
To undo the heavy burdens,
To let the oppressed go free,
And that you break every yoke? (Isa. 58:6)

God will reveal to you through fasting and prayer something that you are to *do*. It may be a change in current behavior, it may be a call to a new behavior. Look for the specific, practical, next-step action that God has for you as you emerge from a time of fasting and prayer. He has a plan and purpose for you to fulfill.

- *What new insights do you have into fasting and prayer?*

_____

_____

- *In what ways are you feeling challenged in your prayer life?*

_____

_____

LESSON 5

A PRAYER BURDEN

In the last lesson, we touched briefly on Nehemiah's response when he heard that his people were in great distress and reproach, the walls of Jerusalem were broken, and the gates of the city were burned:

> I sat down and wept, and mourned for many days. . . . And I said: "I pray, LORD God of heaven, O great and awesome God, You who keep Your covenant and mercy with those who love You and observe Your commandments, please let Your ear be attentive and Your eyes open, that You may hear the prayer of Your servant which I pray before You now, day and night." (Neh. 1:4–6)

Nehemiah was experiencing a prayer burden.

A prayer burden can be defined as *a strong motivation to pray for others and to carry the needs of others before God in prayer until God responds.*

The Bible has a great deal to say about burdens. We are to bear one another's burdens (Gal. 6:2). We are to go the second mile in helping another person (Matt. 5:41). We are subject to God's punishment if we place burdens upon others (Amos 5:11; Matt. 18:6–7). Much of our ability to bear natural burdens is derived from developing our ability to carry spiritual burdens in prayer.

A burden of prayer is marked usually by a sense of spiritual weight—a heaviness of heart, a drag on one's emotions, a spirit of mourning, or a feeling of restlessness that arises because we can't seem to shift ourselves away from a problem or need that has come to our attention.

What the Word Says	What the Word Says to Me
Bear one another's burdens, and so fulfill the law of Christ. (Gal. 6:2)	---------------------------------- ----------------------------------
Whoever compels you to go one mile, go with him two. (Matt. 5:41)	---------------------------------- ----------------------------------
But you, beloved, building yourselves up on your most holy faith, praying in the Holy Spirit, keep yourselves in the love of God, looking for the mercy of our Lord Jesus Christ unto eternal life. And on some have compassion, making a distinction; but others save with fear, pulling them out of the fire. (Jude 20–23)	---------------------------------- ---------------------------------- ---------------------------------- ---------------------------------- ---------------------------------- ---------------------------------- ---------------------------------- ---------------------------------- ---------------------------------- ----------------------------------

- *Can you recall a time in your life when you have experienced a prayer burden? How did the burden feel to you? How did you respond? What was the result?*

_____

_____

The Source of Burdens

Burdens tend to arise from one of three sources. *First, a burden may be the result of a self-inflicted error, sin, or guilt.* This type of burden could be called a "burden of conviction." The Holy Spirit allows us to feel the full weight of our sin and guilt. The antidote for this type of burden is to confess our sin to God, receive His forgiveness, and move forward in our lives, relying on the Holy Spirit to help us turn away from the error or sin that has weighed us down.

Second, a burden may come from the negative thinking or behavior of another person. We may find ourselves depressed under a load of guilt that another person tries to lay on us, or angry over another person's negative behavior. Our best response to this type of burden is to ask

God to deal with the other person, to forgive us for anything we may have done (known or unknown), and to help us withstand the persecution. Jesus gave clear instructions about how we are to deal with those who persecute us: we are to have an attitude of love toward them, pray for them, speak well of them, and do good to them. (See Matt. 5:44.)

Third, a prayer burden may come from God. In these cases, God is desiring to get our attention about something so we will pray about it. The burden may be triggered by something that somebody else says or does. In the case of Nehemiah, God used messengers from Jerusalem to tell Nehemiah about the brokenness of God's people and city. The burden to pray, however, came directly from God. God was calling Nehemiah to zero in on the problems at hand and to pray . . . *so that God could act!*

God does not act in many situations because we do not pray. God gave us free will and He will not override our free will, which includes our ability to choose sin and evil over righteousness and goodness. God waits for either someone who is a co-instigator of the negative situation to cry out to Him for forgiveness or for someone who is the victim of a negative situation to cry out to Him for mercy. Then He will act.

If you are burdened to pray for another person, God desires to act on that person's behalf. He places the burden to pray on your heart so He has an opening in the spirit realm through which to move. As you pray, you are allowed to get in on the blessing that God has for you and for that person through an answered prayer.

All prayer is threefold:

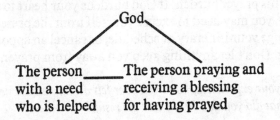

God

The person	The person praying and
with a need	receiving a blessing
who is helped	for having prayed

This triangular aspect of prayer is the way God builds up His people to *be* a people, and not just isolated individuals who are in relationship with Him. God wants us not only to communicate with Him and be in relationship with Him, but to communicate and be in relationship with other people. The hallmark quality of this triangle is to be love.

If God is burdening your heart, He is calling you to get involved in other people's problems and heartaches. This is part of God's teaching you how better to love others. In turn, God will place a burden on other people's hearts to pray for you.

Some people who experience prayer burdens may feel physically sick. When they feel down or weary, they turn to their medicine chest or their easy chair when the proper response would be to pray.

- *What new insights do you have into prayer?*

_____

_____

The Weight of the Burden

The weight of a prayer burden is determined by two things: first, the magnitude of the situation or need. A prayer burden may hit with tremendous force, or it may be of lesser intensity but with a nagging persistence over several days and weeks. Second, the weight of a burden is determined by how quickly God desires to deal with the situation. Some problems are resolved immediately, others take time.

In either case, our response to a prayer burden must be immediate. We need to turn away from our daily routine and pray! Nehemiah's response was to sit down and weep as soon as he experienced his prayer burden. If God burdens your heart to pray about a matter, you may need to excuse yourself from the presence of others, change your itinerary or schedule, or cancel an appointment or meeting. Don't let anything keep you away from prayer.

- *In your experience, have you ever felt an immediate need to pray? What did you do? What was the result?*

_____

_____

An Immediate Response

Let me warn you that the devil will launch every temptation to get you to stop praying and go on about your business. You'll suddenly be reminded of a thousand "important" things you need to do. The phone may ring repeatedly. You may feel guilt pangs because you are not doing your daily chores. If you have a burden to pray, however, the most important thing you can do before God is to obey Him and to pray.

What the Word Says	What the Word Says to Me
Submit to God. Resist the devil and he will flee from you. (James 4:7)	-- -- --
Therefore humble yourselves under the mighty hand of God, that He may exalt you in due time, casting all your care upon Him, for He cares for you. Be sober, be vigilant; because your adversary the devil walks about like a roaring lion, seeking whom he may devour. Resist him, steadfast in the faith. (1 Peter 5:6–9)	-- -- -- -- -- -- -- -- -- --

The Difference Between Worry and a Prayer Burden

You are experiencing worry when the focus of your concern is on *your* need, or on how a particular problem or situation affects you. Worry is always self-centered. A prayer burden is focused on God and what He wants to accomplish in the life of another person or the lives of a group of people.

If you don't know whether you are worried or feeling a prayer burden, ask God to reveal to you the nature of what you are experiencing. If your attention is directed to a particular person or situation, God is calling you to pray for that person. If your attention is solely on yourself and how a problem might affect your life, that's worry.

- *Have you ever experienced a sudden urge to pray for another person? How did you feel? What did you do? What was the result?*

_____

_____

How Long Does a Prayer Burden Last?

The length of time we experience a prayer burden is partly up to us. If we respond immediately to the burden to pray, then God can begin to work in us and through us more quickly. If we disobey or balk at God's prayer burden, the burden is likely to linger on and on . . . until we obey. Sometimes a prayer burden will rest on our hearts for hours, sometimes for months. Nehemiah's prayer burden lasted "many days."

A prayer burden will last as long as it takes for God to get us into a position to hear clearly what He desires us to pray about and toward what end. When we experience a prayer burden, we must listen keenly for Him to tell us how to pray and what to pray for. A burden lifts when all of the preparation is completed so that God can act.

If the burden is related to a situation in our personal lives, then the process may take some time as God sifts us and sands us and prepares us and changes us. If the burden is related to a situation in another person's life, then the burden is likely to last until we pray for precisely what God desires to do and until He has removed all obstacles from the path. That process may involve important interim changes in the life of another person or in the course of a circumstance. In Nehemiah's case, the burden lasted until Nehemiah had prayed precisely for the things God wanted to do and God had changed the heart of the king, through whom the provision was going to be made for Nehemiah to return and rebuild the city.

Always keep in mind that God has good in mind. Prayer is a good work performed on the behalf of others. It yields good results because

God works all things for good to those who love Him (Rom. 8:28). A prayer burden is an invitation to be involved in a good process— one that yields a good harvest in both your life and the lives of those for whom you are praying.

What the Word Says	What the Word Says to Me
In my distress I called upon the LORD, And cried out to my God; He heard my voice from His temple, And my cry came before Him, even to His ears. (Ps. 18:6)	_____ _____ _____ _____ _____ _____ _____
And let us not grow weary while doing good, for in due season we shall reap if we do not lose heart. Therefore, as we have opportunity, let us do good to all, especially to those who are of the household of faith. (Gal. 6:9–10)	_____ _____ _____ _____ _____ _____ _____
Weeping may endure for a night, But joy comes in the morning. (Ps. 30:5)	_____ _____ _____

When to Share a Prayer Burden

If God gives you a burden to pray for a specific person, then you are to pray, not gossip about the person. You must not share the nature of the burden on your heart until you are free of any criticism related to the person for whom you are praying, and until God gives you a green light to go to the person for whom you have felt a burden. Nobody else should be involved. The matter is between you and God and the third party.

Some burdens, however, are collective in nature. For example, each of us should feel a strong burden to pray for the spiritual state of our nation, as well as for groups of fellow believers whom we know are facing trouble, crisis, or a major challenge.

Moses and the children of Israel experienced a collective need in the battle they faced with the Amalekites. Moses knew that his role in the battle was to pray. Aaron and Hur were joined to Moses in this prayer burden. The benefit came to all of God's people as Joshua defeated Amalek. (See Ex. 17:8–13.)

What the Word Says

What the Word Says to Me

Now Amalek came and fought with Israel in Rephidim. And Moses said to Joshua, "Choose us some men and go out, fight with Amalek. Tomorrow I will stand on the top of the hill with the rod of God in my hand." So Joshua did as Moses said to him, and fought with Amalek. And Moses, Aaron, and Hur went up to the top of the hill. And so it was, when Moses held up his hand, that Israel prevailed; and when he let down his hand, Amalek prevailed. But Moses' hands became heavy; so they took a stone and put it under him, and he sat on it. And Aaron and Hur supported his hands, one on one side, and the other on the other side; and his hands were steady until the going down of the sun. So Joshua defeated Amalek and his people with the edge of the sword. (Ex. 17:8–13)

The Results of a Prayer Burden

A prayer burden is one of God's methods of cleansing us. As we yield to His call to pray, we will become stripped of self-centeredness. As we pray, we put ourselves in a position to receive a blessing and to have our faith renewed and strengthened. We grow in our awareness of God's methods and His plans. Ultimately, we become a force for bringing about the victory of God over evil. We become agents for good change and increased righteousness.

- *What new insights do you have into God's use of prayer burdens?*

_____

_____

- *In what ways are you being challenged in your prayer life?*

_____

_____

LESSON 6

GETTING ANSWERS TO PRAYER

$\mathbf{M}$any people think that the only answered prayers are those that God answers with a yes. We discussed in an earlier lesson that God sometimes answers us with no and wait. God's answers are always for our good, and they inevitably call us to grow in our faith and to walk more closely with Christ. Nevertheless, we desire God to say yes in answer to our petitions.

We must recognize at the outset that God does not answer our prayers on the basis of our self-worth or our accomplishments. In other words, we cannot earn a yes answer from God. His answers are not granted on the basis of our being good in our own human nature. Rather, God's basis for answering our prayer is His love. If we ever doubt this we need only to look to the Cross. God sent His only Son, Jesus Christ, to die for our sins so that we might be restored to Him in loving fellowship and live with Him forever in heaven (John 3:16).

God gives His children the desires of their hearts if the desires of their hearts are within the parameters of God's will. If you delight in the things of God you will desire to do God's will. God will quickly give you your desires because they are His own for your life.

When we ask something of God, He says yes to us if it will build us up, lead us to eternal life, and help us to be more fruitful witnesses for Him on earth. He knows what is best for us. He will only give what is useful and beneficial for us and for those with whom we have a relationship.

Avoiding the Two Extremes

Many people think that God desires for them to live in poverty. They deny their needs and shun possessions in an effort to increase their faith. The fact is, God delights in providing us what we need. We are to receive God's blessings with a spirit of gratitude. We may enjoy possessions but we do not place our trust in them. Our loving heavenly Father does not want us to live with great areas of need in our lives. That brings no glory to Him.

At the other extreme are people who think that God should give them everything they want at the snap of their fingers. The reality is that there are certain things that God does not grant to us for our good. If He granted all of our requests, we could easily become greedy and lose sight of His call for us to help others who are in need.

God balances His giving to us. He desires that we walk in close relationship with Him, trusting Him to meet our needs and to equip us fully in every area of our lives to do the work He is calling us to do.

Prerequisites for Yes Answers

In the Scriptures God has outlined five prerequisites for receiving yes answers to our prayers.

1. Right Relationship

God wants us to live in a right relationship with Him and with others. Of course, at times we slip and cause our relationships with Him and others to be strained. We are human beings and we have a great capacity to fail and to err. God knows that.

God does not look at our track record nearly as much as He looks at our motivation—are our aim and desire to love and serve Him? If so, God will correct us and continue to hear our prayers and answer them with yes. Those who truly have a heart for God often fail and pick themselves up and try again, and fail and pick themselves up and try again. All the while, God knows they are desiring to move ever closer to Him and to serve Him to the best of their ability. Such people receive many yes answers to their prayers.

If our aim, however, is to continue willfully in sin and to ignore God's attempts at correcting us, then God is under no obligation to hear and answer us. We are choosing to pursue our own self-interests, which God knows inevitably will lead to our downfall. God will not contribute to anything that will be a negative to our spiritual growth or cause pain to others.

What the Word Says	What the Word Says to Me
If I regard iniquity in my heart, The Lord will not hear. (Ps. 66:18)	
When You said, "Seek My face," My heart said to You, "Your face, LORD, I will seek." Do not hide Your face from me; Do not turn Your servant away in anger; You have been my help; Do not leave me nor forsake me, O God of my salvation.... Teach me Your way, O LORD, And lead me in a smooth path. (Ps. 27:8–9, 11)	

- *In your life, have you ever asked God for something that you knew was contrary to righteousness? What was the result?*

_____

_____

2. Right Method

God does not give us a universal formula for making our petitions, but He does ask us to be definite and specific in our prayers. He also tells us to ask with thanksgiving and with faith.

Some people pray, "God, bless the nation; God, bless the church; God, bless my family," but what do they mean? How do they define *blessing?* Nobody would say to a waitress in a restaurant, "I want food and drink." When we order in a restaurant, we make a specific request. I know people who say, "Well, God can read my mind and my heart. He knows what I want." My response to them is, "If you have a blank mind, what is God reading?" When Jesus approached Bartimaeus, a man He obviously could tell was blind, He asked him, "What do you want Me to do for you?" (Mark 10:51). Jesus asks the same question of us.

We are also to pray with thanksgiving. Our praise and thanksgiving to God are direct reflections of our faith—we are saying to God, "I know, Lord, that You are working all things together for my good and that You will grant me only what is for my eternal benefit. I thank You for giving me precisely what I need, when I need it, and in the proper way. I am voicing to You my desires for what I believe is best for me, but I thank You for hearing me and granting to me what You know to be the best for me."

What the Word Says

Be anxious for nothing, but in everything by prayer and supplication, with thanksgiving, let your requests be made known to God. (Phil. 4:6)

Therefore I say to you, whatever things you ask when you pray, believe that you receive them, and you will have them. (Mark 11:24)

Ask, and you will receive, that your joy may be full. (John 16:24)

What the Word Says to Me

• *How do you feel when you ask something specifically and directly of God? How do you feel when you pray with thanksgiving?*

----

3. Right Requests

If we desire to receive a yes answer from God, the request that we make of God must be according to His will (1 John 5:14). God has a plan and a purpose for your life. He sees precisely what will be involved and required for that purpose to be fulfilled—today, tomorrow, next year, and on down the path of your life. He will not grant you a petition that causes you to stray from that plan.

On the night before His crucifixion, Jesus prayed in the Garden of Gethsemane, "Not as I will, but as You will" (Matt. 26:39). Jesus did not want to stray even one degree from God's perfect plan for His life. His prayer must become our prayer. Then, and only then, can we be assured of continual yes answers.

God's plan for us includes timing. Some things may be right for us, but not right now. When we pray, "Your will, not mine," we must be aware that we are also praying, "Your timing, not mine."

What the Word Says	What the Word Says to Me
Now this is the confidence that we have in Him, that if we ask anything according to His will, He hears us. And if we know that He hears us, whatever we ask, we know that we have the petitions that we have asked of Him. (1 John 5:14–15)	_____
Every purpose of the LORD shall be performed. (Jer. 51:29)	_____
To everything there is a season, A time for every purpose under heaven. . . . God shall judge the righteous and the wicked, For there is a time there for every purpose and for every work. (Eccl. 3:1, 17)	_____

• *In your past experience, have you had a time when you knew God was answering you with a resounding yes? On what did you base your knowledge? What was the result?*

_____

_____

4. Right Framework

Although there is no formula for prayer, there is a framework. Our prayers are to be voiced in the name of Jesus.

Many people close all of their prayers with the phrase, "in the name of Jesus, amen." Some do this as if this phrase is a magic tag to get what they want. Nothing could be farther from the truth of God. Others take God's promises regarding the name of Jesus to mean that they can ask for anything they want and then seal it with the name of Jesus to ensure they get it. They look for a particular Scripture that seems to assure them of a promise of God and then claim it "in the name of Jesus" for themselves. They are asking amiss. The emphasis must always be on our residing and abiding fully in the name of Jesus and not on the request we make!

To pray in the name of Jesus means to pray as if Jesus Himself were voicing the prayer. To be "in His name" is to have so buried our identity in His identity that we are totally and completely covered with Christ. To any observer in the heavenly realm, we are operating as if Christ Himself were acting or speaking.

What we ask in Jesus' name must be completely in character with what Jesus would ask if He were walking in our shoes, living our lives, going where we go, and meeting whom we meet. What would Jesus need? What would Jesus desire? These are the things that we are to request in Jesus' name. When we do, we are in the proper position to receive a yes answer from God.

What the Word Says	What the Word Says to Me
And whatever you ask in My name, that I will do, that the Father may be glorified in the	_____ _____ _____

Son. If you ask anything in My
name, I will do it. (John
14:13–14)

I chose you and appointed you that
you should go and bear fruit, and
that your fruit should remain, that
whatever you ask the Father in My
name He may give you. (John
15:16)

- *What new insights do you have into praying in the name of Jesus?*

5. Right Attitude

We are always to make our petitions without doubt. Our attitude must be one of faith. Many people ask God for things but the tone of their voice conveys, "Oh, but I'm not worthy of this." Perhaps they are attempting to be humble, but if so, they are displaying a false humility. God calls us to make our petitions boldly and in faith, without doubt.

On what do we base our faith? On the fact that God wants only what is best for us. If we ask for what we are certain God desires for us, we must ask as if we are already in the process of receiving it. You may say, "But what if I am asking for the wrong thing?" If you are, and you are asking in the context of a right relationship and framework, being specific and definite and thankful, and asking to the best of your understanding of God's will . . . then the Lord will show you if you are asking in error. You aren't omniscient and God doesn't expect you to be. What He does expect of you is that you operate in the fullness of your present level of understanding and faith, and also with an open heart for Him to correct you and guide you into the *precision of perfection* that He desires for you. If you come to Him with that attitude, He will grant you many yes answers, and He will lead you to ask only for those things that He can answer with a *yes!*

What the Word Says	What the Word Says to Me
If any of you lacks wisdom, let him ask of God, who gives to all liberally and without reproach, and it will be given to him. But let him ask in faith, with no doubting, for he who doubts is like a wave of the sea driven and tossed by the wind. For let not that man suppose that he will receive anything from the Lord; he is a double-minded man, unstable in all his ways. (James 1:5–8)	-------------------------- -------------------------- -------------------------- -------------------------- -------------------------- -------------------------- -------------------------- -------------------------- -------------------------- -------------------------- --------------------------
I thank my God always concerning you for the grace of God which was given to you by Christ Jesus, that you were enriched in everything by Him in all utterance and all knowledge, even as the testimony of Christ was confirmed in you, so that you come short in no gift, eagerly waiting for the revelation of our Lord Jesus Christ, who will also confirm you to the end, that you may be blameless in the day of our Lord Jesus Christ. (1 Cor. 1:4–8)	-------------------------- -------------------------- -------------------------- -------------------------- -------------------------- -------------------------- -------------------------- -------------------------- -------------------------- -------------------------- -------------------------- -------------------------- -------------------------- -------------------------- --------------------------

- *In what ways are you challenged in your prayer life today?*

All for God's Glory

When we voice our prayers out of a right relationship with God and in a definite, specific and thankful way, and we know that our attitude is right ... to a very great extent we can be assured that we are praying in Jesus' name and that our requests will be in keeping with God's will. Each of the five prerequisites to yes answers works together with all of the others. For example, a right attitude flows from a right relationship. A right request is best voiced with the right method. The right framework is directly linked to a right relationship.

The reason God says yes to our prayers is not only that we might find fulfillment and meaning and joy in our lives, but also that God might be glorified. Jesus said, "Let your light so shine before men, that they may see your good works and glorify your Father in heaven" (Matt. 5:16). When nonbelievers see us living in right relationship with God and God answering our prayers, they are drawn to God. They desire to know Him better and to receive more fully from Him.

God desires to say yes to you when you pray. We must make it our desire to pray in such a way that He will say yes to us.

- *What new insights do you have into receiving God's yes answers to your prayers?*

———————————————————————————

———————————————————————————

LESSON 7

PRAYING IN THE WILL OF GOD

In the last lesson, we touched briefly on the necessity for our prayers to be according to God's will. Many of us struggle with knowing God's will. We have no difficulty with the big picture—that we accept Christ Jesus as Savior and follow Him as our Lord, that we do good works, keep God's commandments, and be active in our witness as the Holy Spirit leads and guides us on a daily basis. We struggle, rather, with how to make daily decisions and choices regarding our families, jobs, church commitments, and friendships. In other words, we usually know how to pray about the eternal issues, but we're unsure about daily, practical matters.

In 1 John 5:14–15, we read,

> Now this is the confidence that we have in Him, that if we ask anything according to His will, He hears us. And if we know that He hears us, whatever we ask, we know that we have the petitions that we have asked of Him.

This passage of Scripture bears a threefold promise to believers:

1. God hears us when we pray according to His will.
2. We will possess what we request if we ask according to His will.
3. We will *know* that we will possess what we ask if we ask according to His will.

When we have the confidence of knowing that God is granting our petitions, we have a great boldness and freedom. Note, too, that these verses deal with our personal requests. Some people believe that they are being proud or presumptuous in asking God to meet their personal needs. That opinion is not scriptural. God wants you always to ask for the things you want, need, or desire.

God Wants Us to Know

The passage in 1 John assures us that we can pray about anything. No issue, situation, relationship, circumstance, or possession is too big or too small to bring to God in prayer. This passage also conveys to us the truth that we *can* know the will of God. If it was impossible for us to know the will of God, these verses would be null and void of meaning. To the contrary, they encourage us to seek God's will and to live within it. The will of God is what is *pleasing to God* and *according to God's purposes.*

Can we know everything that God purposes? No. God's ways are higher than our ways. (See Isa. 55:8–9.) God is omniscient and eternal. He knows things, has plans and purposes, and is operating on a timetable that we can never know fully. What we can be assured of is this: *we can know precisely what God purposes for us to the degree that God desires for us to know.* We can count on God to reveal to us all of the information that we need to have in order to defeat the devil and to fulfill God's plan for our lives. We cannot know all of God's purposes, but we can know the ones that directly involve us. In other words, we can know if we should marry a certain person, buy a certain car, take a certain job, invest in a particular opportunity, or make other decisions that directly involve us.

Furthermore, if we don't know how to pray about a specific area or situation in our lives, we can trust the Holy Spirit who resides within us to guide our prayers so that we will know the mind of God, even as the Spirit knows the mind of God. (See Rom. 8:26–27.) The Father wants us to have spiritual understanding and practical wisdom.

What the Word Says	What the Word Says to Me
For this reason we also, since the	------------------------------

day we heard it, do not cease to pray for you, and to ask that you may be filled with the knowledge of His will in all wisdom and spiritual understanding; that you may walk worthy of the Lord, fully pleasing Him, being fruitful in every good work and increasing in the knowledge of God; strengthened with all might, according to His glorious power, for all patience and longsuffering with joy; giving thanks to the Father who has qualified us to be partakers of the inheritance of the saints in the light. (Col. 1:9–12)

If any of you lacks wisdom, let him ask of God, who gives to all liberally and without reproach, and it will be given to him. (James 1:5)

Likewise the Spirit also helps in our weaknesses. For we do not know what we should pray for as we ought, but the Spirit Himself makes intercession for us with groanings which cannot be uttered. Now He who searches the hearts knows what the mind of the Spirit is, because He makes intercession for the saints according to the will of God. (Rom. 8:26–27)

- *How do you feel about the promise of God that you can know His will?*

Not a Blanket Statement

Sometimes when we pray, "If it is Your will," we do so because we don't want to take the time or make the effort to know God's will. The verses we often use to justify this approach are Matthew 26:39, 42: "O My Father, if it is possible, let this cup pass from Me; nevertheless, not as I will, but as You will. . . . O My Father, if this cup cannot pass away from Me unless I drink it, Your will be done." What we wrongly assume from these verses is that Jesus didn't know God's will, and therefore, He prayed, "Your will be done." Or some of us may believe that Jesus really didn't want to do God's will and die on the cross, and therefore, He was asking God to change His mind, but was willing to accept God's purpose for His life if God didn't change His mind. That is not what these verses are saying.

Jesus knew that He had to die on the cross. The cup to which Jesus referred was not the Cross. He had told His disciples about His death repeatedly as they made their plans to come to Jerusalem in the weeks before His crucifixion. He made it very clear that He had to suffer at the hands of the religious leadership, be crucified, and that He would rise again the third day. He knew fully and clearly that God's purpose for Him was to die a sacrificial death at precisely the right time so that all of the Scriptures concerning the "Lamb slain from the foundation of the world" would be fulfilled. (See Rev. 13:8.) He knew He had to die in Jerusalem, at the time of Passover.

What "cup" was Jesus desiring to have pass from Him? Jesus knew that if He bore the sin of the world on the cross, He and the Father would be separated for a period of time because the Father could not look on sin. To be separated from the Father, even for a fraction of a second, was an unthinkable thought for Jesus. He had never been separated from the Father for even one moment in all of eternity up to that point. His request of God was that if there was any way that this aspect of the Cross might be altered, He desired for it to be altered.

God desires for us to know His will and to pray within His will. We are not to pray for anything that pops into our minds and then tack on the statement "if it is Your will," assuming then that if we get what we wish for it is God's will, and if we don't get what we wish for it isn't. This kind of prayer signifies an immature relationship with our heavenly Father. God desires, rather, that our relationship with Him be so personal and intimate that we *know* His will and are bold to claim it.

* *What new insights do you have into the issue of praying according to God's will?*

_____

_____

What About Fleeces?

Some of us determine God's will by "throwing fleeces." In other words, we take the attitude, "If X happens, then I'll do one thing, but if Z happens, then I'll do another." This is similar to tossing the will of God like a coin and basing our decisions on whether it falls heads or tails.

The act of fleece-throwing is found in the book of Judges, where Gideon is called by God to engage in battle with the Midianites. (See Judg. 6:36–40.) I want to point out three things about this practice. First, the fleece-throwing was Gideon's idea, not God's. Nowhere in Scripture does God authorize this as a desirable method for knowing His purposes. Second, this is the only time in Scripture when the method was used. It was not employed by any other person. And third, the fleece-throwing was not performed to know God's will, but to gain confidence in the outcome that God had promised. Gideon already knew with certainty that it was the will of God that he lead the people into battle against the Midianites. The armies had already been gathered for that battle. Gideon knew he was the leader. He was asking God for a sign that he and the Israelites were going to be successful.

Repeatedly in the Scriptures God calls us to be faithful to Him without regard to whether we will be successful. True trust in God is to follow Him wherever He leads and to do whatever He directs without any concern for the outcome. Gideon's fleece-throwing was a sign that he didn't trust God. Likewise today in many cases, fleece-throwing is used by people who don't really trust God to be true to His word.

- *Have you ever given God an either-or choice in answering your prayers? What new insights do you have into this approach to knowing God's will?*

An Approach to Knowing God's Will

Throughout this book, I am assuming that you are in right relationship with God as you approach God in prayer. A right relationship with God is imperative for you to be able to discern the will of God. If you have not accepted Jesus as your Savior, you do not have the Holy Spirit residing in you to guide your prayers and to prompt you in right directions and choices. If you are in willful disobedience to God, the foremost will of God for your life is that you confess your disobedience, repent of your sin, receive His forgiveness, and obey Him. All other requests for discernment are subject to your willingness to obey and do what God reveals to you to do.

On the other hand, if you are in right relationship with God, you are likely to find that the threefold approach described below will be useful to you as you seek to know God's will.

1. Distinguish Among Need, Desire, and Opportunity

What circumstance are you facing and how does it make you feel? Do you need a specific amount of money? Then you have a need. Do you have a longing to be married to a particular person? Then you have a desire. Are you being approached about a change in your employment? Then you are facing opportunity.

The Bible clearly states that God wants to help you with your needs, desires, and decisions regarding opportunities. Steep yourself in the verses that promise you His help and provision.

What the Word Says	What the Word Says to Me
God shall supply all your need according to His riches in glory by Christ Jesus. (Phil. 4:19)	-----
Delight yourself also in the LORD, And He shall give you the desires of your heart. Commit your way to the LORD, Trust also in Him, And He shall bring it to pass. (Ps. 37:4–5)	-----
Wait on the LORD, And keep His way, And He shall exalt you to inherit the land. (Ps. 37:34)	-----
The LORD is my shepherd; I shall not want. He makes me to lie down in green pastures; He leads me beside the still waters. He restores my soul; He leads me in the paths of righteousness For His name's sake. (Ps. 23:1–3)	-----

2. Find a Biblical Example

Ask God to reveal to you a passage of Scripture that addresses the situation you are facing. The Bible is filled with examples that cover the entire range of human need, desires, and opportunities. You may come across such an example as part of your daily reading of God's Word. Or you may need to engage in a specific Bible study on the matter, using a concordance and spending a concentrated amount of time in searching the Scriptures until you find one or more biblical examples that address the issue you are facing or the feelings you are experiencing.

Once you have a Scripture example, don't read just one verse and then say, "Aha! Here's my answer." Meditate on the entire passage of Scripture that seems to pertain to your situation. This is critically important because the meditation process is a sifting, refining process. Ponder over a period of time what God is saying and relate that truth to other areas of His Word in which He has conveyed a similar message. Take some time to *know* what God is saying, and specifically, what He seems to be saying to you.

Then go to God in prayer. Say, "Lord, I trust You to give me Your wisdom according to James 1:5. I trust that the Holy Spirit will help me to pray as I should pray according to Romans 8:26–27. I have found this example in Your Word that seems to relate to my situation. I want to do Your will and I submit myself totally to You. On the basis of Your word to me and my desire to follow You, I'm coming to You right now with this particular need [or desire or opportunity], and I am asking You to meet my need [answer my desire, or help me make a choice regarding this opportunity]."

Pray with faith! Thank God for giving you His wisdom and answering your prayer. Believe that you have God's full assurance that you will know His will and that He is going to grant your petition. Claim that this is going to be done in God's timing and start thanking Him for doing it. You don't need to know all the details about how and when God is going to act. Start thanking Him now for giving you the assurance that He is going to meet your need, guide you in your desire, or help you in responding to an opportunity.

- *Recall at least one experience in your life in which you felt a close kinship with what a Bible character was thinking or feeling. What confidence did you draw from that example?*

---

3. Ask God to Reveal the Path You Should Take

If you are facing two or more equally good choices, ask God to reveal specifically which path you should take. Again, find a Scripture passage that relates to the situation you are facing. Claim God's guidance for your life, then pray, "Show me how to pray and what to choose. I'll obey You fully as You reveal to me what to do."

Often when we pray this way, God will reveal to us yet another way that is the perfect path. Sometimes He will make it clear that He favors one particular way. Other times God leaves the choice to us. Either way is acceptable to Him as part of His will, and He gives us free reign to choose.

The key is to wait until we know with certainty how God wants us to respond. This is important. We often come to a full understanding of the situation or a full knowledge of God's answer *as we wait*. We meditate about the situation in prayer over several hours or days, and we consider carefully what the Spirit is speaking in our hearts. We don't rush to a conclusion or decision or act until we know with certainty that we have heard from God.

Enveloped in Peace

God's perfect plan and purposes for our lives will envelop us in peace. We will have a feeling of resolution in our hearts. We will feel great peace of mind. When we feel confused, unsettled, fearful, troubled, or uneasy about the decision we have made after following this Bible-based process, then we are not experiencing God's direction. Knowing His will allows us always to move calmly and with confidence, even in desperate situations or in the face of enormous challenges.

What the Word Says	What the Word Says to Me
Trust in the LORD with all your heart, And lean not on your own understanding; In all your ways acknowledge Him, And He shall direct your paths. (Prov. 3:5–6)	_____ _____ _____ _____ _____ _____ _____
The peace of God, which surpasses all understanding, will guard your	_____

hearts and minds through Christ
Jesus. (Phil. 4:7)

[Jesus said]: "The Helper, the
Holy Spirit, whom the Father will
send in My name, He will teach
you all things, and bring to your
remembrance all things that I said
to you. Peace I leave with you, My
peace I give to you.... Let not
your heart be troubled, neither let
it be afraid." (John 14:26–27)

• *In what ways are you being challenged in your prayer life?*

LESSON 8

WHY PRAYERS AREN'T ANSWERED

When our prayers aren't answered in the way we want—generally speaking, when we receive a wait or a no answer—we sometimes become discouraged, perhaps even resentful. What we fail to recognize is that wait and no answers are tremendous teaching tools. Any serious student will admit that he or she has learned a lot from mistakes made on an exam. Our failures in life are very often our greatest teachers. So, too, with God's wait and no answers. They can reveal to us what actions we should take or how we should grow in our relationship with the Lord.

In this lesson we will focus on God's wait and no answers to see what they might tell us. Again, I am assuming that you are in right relationship with God. The person who has not accepted Jesus Christ as Savior or who is in willful rebellion against God is not a person who can expect yes answers from God. God's answer is likely to be a repeated no until the person surrenders his or her life fully to Christ. Being a believer, however, and even desiring to live in right relationship with God does not always ensure that we will have all of our prayers answered with a yes. There are certain practical and specific reasons why God doesn't always say yes to Christians.

God's Wait Answer

God desires for us to want Him more than we want any person, position, or object. He wants us to trust Him explicitly and fully. He wants us to be in a deep, personal, and intimate relationship with Him, totally relying upon Him to meet our needs and guide us on a daily basis.

Sometimes God answers wait so that we will refocus totally upon God and not on the object of our desire. God wants us to see Him as the source of our supply and know that a relationship with Him is far more valuable than any answered prayer could ever be.

Sometimes God answers wait so that we might trust Him more fully. If God immediately said yes to all of our prayers, we might soon think that His answers were based on our own righteousness, rather than upon His mercy and grace. In giving us wait answers, God is building into us a stronger foundation of faith, one that will endure all persecutions and trials.

Sometimes God answers wait so that our attitude will be adjusted and refined to more accurately reflect the attitude of Christ Jesus. God may need for us to have a different attitude so that we will know how best to use the blessing He is about to give us. At other times, we must mature in some way so that we can handle the blessing. A young child may want a pocketknife, but a wise parent knows that a pocketknife is not an appropriate gift for a young child. The parent waits until the child is older and can use the pocketknife properly without causing injury to himself or others. Likewise, God may delay His answer to our prayer until we are better prepared to accept it.

Sometimes God answers wait because certain aspects of God's desire for us are yet to be put into place. Another person or group of people may be involved in the blessing. God may need to work in their hearts before He can give us what He desires us to have. He needs to remove the hindrances that keep His will from being enacted. To "hinder" literally means to break up, or to place an obstacle in the road, so that our way is impeded. God may need to do some "removal work" in the heart of another person before that person can share in our blessing.

Finally, God sometimes answers wait because He is preparing for an even greater blessing than the one for which we asked. This certainly was true in the case of Lazarus. Jesus knew that Lazarus was ill, and He could have gone to him to heal him before he died. Instead, Jesus waited until Lazarus had died so that He might raise him from the dead as a definitive sign of His authority over death and the assurance of our resurrection in Christ. (See John 11:1–45.)

- *Have you ever experienced a wait answer from the Lord? Do you have an understanding as to why God gave that answer?*

What the Word Says	What the Word Says to Me
I am the LORD your God, who brought you out of the land of Egypt, out of the house of bondage. You shall have no other gods before Me.... For I, the LORD your God, am a jealous God. (Ex. 20:2–3, 5)	
It is better to trust in the LORD Than to put confidence in man. It is better to trust in the LORD Than to put confidence in princes. (Ps. 118:8–9)	
The loftiness of man shall be bowed down, And the haughtiness of men shall be brought low; The LORD alone will be exalted in that day, But the idols He shall utterly abolish. (Isa. 2:17–18)	
You will keep him in perfect peace, Whose mind is stayed on You, Because he trusts in You. Trust in the LORD forever, For in YAH, the LORD, is everlasting strength. (Isa. 26:3–4)	

For since the beginning of the
world

Men have not heard nor perceived
by the ear,

Nor has the eye seen any God
besides You,

Who acts for the one who waits for
Him. (Isa. 64:4)

----

* *How do you feel when God tells you to wait?*

_____

_____

* *What new insights do you have into the reasons for God's wait answers?*

_____

_____

* *In what ways are you being challenged in your prayer life?*

_____

_____

God's No Answers

When we hear about someone receiving an answer of no from God, our first impulse may be to assume that there is sin in that person's life. Likewise, when we are the ones receiving the no answer, we may assume that sin is the cause, and we may try to argue that point with God or justify our position and request. The greater reality, however, is that we probably are in *error*, not sin, and God is using a no answer to correct our error.

Sin is willful disobedience against what we know God desires. Sin, especially on the part of a believer in Jesus Christ, is a matter of saying, "I know what God's commandments say, but I choose to do otherwise." It is a deliberate act of rebellion and defiance. We experience a breach in our relationship with God and the Holy Spirit moves to convict us of our sin, usually with increasing intensity.

Error, in contrast, is an unknowing, inadvertent, unwillful disobedience. We do not know we are making an incorrect choice or engaging in unrighteous behavior because we have not been taught that what we are doing is wrong in God's eyes. We desire a relationship with God and will be quick to amend our ways once we realize our error . . . but at present, we do not know that we are erring. God's no answer is a means of bringing us to the point where we recognize our error so we can correct our behavior. Once we correct our behavior, God's answer to our same petition may very well be yes.

There are at least six areas of error that evoke a no answer from God.

1. Relationships Are Not Right Before God

One reason God gives us an answer of no is that our relationships with other people are not right.

Our heavenly Father always forgives, is merciful, and desires the best for us. He will not answer our prayers as long as we remain unforgiving, unmerciful, or self-centered and demanding of those He has given us as marriage partners, family members, and friends. We cannot be caustic, sarcastic, cynical, mean-spirited, resentful, or selfish to other people and then come to the Father and expect Him to answer all of our petitions. He has clearly said that we must forgive if we are to be forgiven. We must be givers before we expect to receive. (See Luke 6:37–38.)

In 1 Peter 3:1–7, we find a balanced approach to the relationship that God desires for a husband and wife to have. Peter says that if this relationship is not in right balance, our prayers are hindered. Your relationship must be right with your spouse for God to answer your prayers, because in marriage, two people are made one and are regarded as one flesh by God. God will not answer your prayer unless He is fully assured that His answer is going to be a blessing that you are going to share fully with your spouse. Your request to God must be one that honors and considers your spouse and is generous toward your spouse.

What the Word Says	What the Word Says to Me
Husbands, likewise, dwell with [your wives] with understanding, giving honor to the wife, as to the weaker vessel, and as being heirs	_____ _____ _____ _____

together of the grace of life, that
your prayers may not be hindered.
(1 Peter 3:7)

Judge not, and you shall not be
judged. Condemn not, and you
shall not be condemned. Forgive,
and you will be forgiven. Give, and
it will be given to you: good measure, pressed down, shaken
together, and running over will be
put into your bosom. For with the
same measure that you use, it will
be measured back to you. (Luke
6:37–38)

If you forgive men their trespasses,
your heavenly Father will also forgive you. But if you do not forgive
men their trespasses, neither will
your Father forgive your trespasses. (Matt. 6:14–15)

2. Motive Is for Self Alone

A second reason why God gives us answers of no is that our request
is totally self-serving. The epistle of James says, "You ask and do not
receive, because you ask amiss, that you may spend it on your plea-
sures" (4:3).

All of our actions as Christians are either aimed at self or God.
Our motive is either to exalt ourselves or to bring glory to God. In
serving others, we bring glory to God, so we might say our actions
are motivated either by a desire to serve self or others.

God gives us a no answer so that we can confront our own motives.
Why are we asking God for a certain thing or situation? Is it so that
we will look better, feel better, or get more praise from other people?
Or is it so we might help others better and be better able to fulfill
the destiny that God has laid before us? God will not answer our
prayers unless He is certain that we will be good stewards of the
things He gives to us and that we will be generous to others.

Very specifically, God expects us to be generous to those who are in need. Many of God's blessings in the Bible are reserved for those who take care of the poor, the widows, and the orphans. We must use what God gives us to bring about justice and equity for those who are lacking the basic essentials of life.

What the Word Says	What the Word Says to Me
Pride goes before destruction, And a haughty spirit before a fall. (Prov. 16:18)	------------------------ ------------------------ ------------------------
He who loves pleasure will be a poor man; He who loves wine and oil will not be rich. (Prov. 21:17)	------------------------ ------------------------ ------------------------ ------------------------
Therefore hear this now, you who are given to pleasures, Who dwell securely, Who say in your heart, "I am, and there is no one else besides me." . . . Therefore evil shall come upon you; You shall not know from where it arises. And trouble shall fall upon you; You will not be able to put it off. (Isa. 47:8, 11)	------------------------ ------------------------ ------------------------ ------------------------ ------------------------ ------------------------ ------------------------ ------------------------ ------------------------ ------------------------ ------------------------ ------------------------
Whoever shuts his ears to the cry of the poor Will also cry himself and not be heard. (Prov. 21:13)	------------------------ ------------------------ ------------------------ ------------------------

3. Wavering Faith

Another reason why God says no to our prayers is because we are wishy-washy in our faith. God has little regard for faith that wavers—a faith that says, "Maybe God will, maybe He won't." Such faith is unstable and unreliable.

God sometimes gives us an answer of no so we will reevaluate our opinion of God and also come to grips with our own emotions. Many people are driven by their emotions. One day they claim to feel God's presence and they have joy and peace. The next day, when they are a little down or discouraged, they say they don't feel God's presence and therefore God must not care about them. They become resentful and bitter toward God. God, however, hasn't changed. Their emotional temperament is being tossed about like wind-driven waves.

Our relationship with God must be based squarely on what the Bible says God desires for us and has given to us through Jesus Christ. We are not to base our relationship with God on how we feel on any given day. Feelings come and go. God's Word remains. Our prayers must be grounded in the Word, not in ourselves.

What the Word Says	What the Word Says to Me
Let him ask in faith, with no doubting, for he who doubts is like a wave of the sea driven and tossed by the wind. For let not that man suppose that he will receive anything from the Lord; he is a double-minded man, unstable in all his ways. (James 1:6–7)	_____
Jesus Christ is the same yesterday, today, and forever. Do not be carried about with various and strange doctrines. For it is good that the heart be established by grace. (Heb. 13:8–9)	_____

4. A Failure to Tithe

One of the most common yet unrecognized errors that can bring about a no answer from God is our failure to tithe. God does not tolerate stinginess—whether toward Him or toward other people.

If God does not seem to be answering your request for things, money, or material goods, check your giving. It may be God is seeking to teach you a new set of priorities in your handling of money. He may be attempting to give you a new understanding of stewardship.

God will not violate the cycle of giving that He established for humankind: giving, receiving, giving, receiving. His law is one that requires reciprocity.

What the Word Says	What the Word Says to Me
"Bring all the tithes into the storehouse, That there may be food in My house, And try Me now in this," Says the LORD of hosts, "If I will not open for you the windows of heaven And pour out for you such blessing That there will not be room enough to receive it." (Mal. 3:10)	------------------------------- ------------------------------- ------------------------------- ------------------------------- ------------------------------- ------------------------------- ------------------------------- ------------------------------- ------------------------------- -------------------------------
All the tithe of the land . . . is the LORD's. It is holy to the LORD. (Lev. 27:30)	------------------------------- ------------------------------- -------------------------------

5. Indifference to God's Word

Sometimes God gives us an answer of no so that we will get serious about reading His Word and applying it to our lives. You cannot live with a closed Bible and expect to have an open line to heaven.

The Bible is God's manual for right living. It contains His promises related to prayer and the meeting of our needs. It holds God's commandments for how to receive and use God's blessings and defeat the enemy of our souls. We cannot turn a deaf ear to God's Word and then approach God with our requests. That would be like a college student telling his professors, "I don't need to attend classes or study any courses. Just give me a degree and I'll be on my way." Can you imagine the response that student would receive?

The Bible has both information and inspiration that you need for your daily walk with God. Avail yourself of it. You'll gain important insights into how to pray so that you get yes answers from God.

What the Word Says	What the Word Says to Me
One who turns away his ear from hearing the law, Even his prayer is an abomination. (Prov. 28:9)	------------------------------- ------------------------------- ------------------------------- -------------------------------
Your word is a lamp to my feet And a light to my path. (Ps. 119:105)	------------------------------- ------------------------------- -------------------------------

6. Unconfessed Sins

God sometimes gives answers of no in response to our unconfessed sins. Just recognizing our errors and sins is not enough. We must confess them to God and receive His forgiveness. It is not sufficient that we recognize that our relationships are wrong, we have failed to tithe, we have wavering faith, we are selfish, or we are indifferent to God's Word. We must actually confess these errors to God and then repent of them, which means to make a willful decision to change. God cannot give us yes answers if we only recognize our errors but do not obey Him and change our ways.

What the Word Says	What the Word Says to Me
Behold, the LORD's hand is not shortened, That it cannot save; Nor His ear heavy, That it cannot hear. But your iniquities have separated you from your God; And your sins have hidden His face from you, So that He will not hear. For your hands are defiled with	------------------------------- ------------------------------- ------------------------------- ------------------------------- ------------------------------- ------------------------------- ------------------------------- ------------------------------- -------------------------------

blood,
And your fingers with iniquity;
Your lips have spoken lies,
Your tongue has muttered perversity. (Isa. 59:1–3)

- *Have you ever experienced a no answer from God? Do you have an understanding as to why God may have said no to you?*

God Desires to Say Yes

God's foremost desire is not to give us answers of wait or no, but to say "yes" to us. Deuteronomy 28 is an important chapter for us to read and study. It tells us that God desires to bless us:

> *Now it shall come to pass, if you diligently obey the voice of the LORD your God, to observe carefully all His commandments which I command you today, that the LORD your God will set you high above all nations of the earth. And all these blessings shall come upon you and overtake you, because you obey the voice of the LORD your God. (vv. 1–2)*

God's desire is for blessing, but if His people turn to follow other gods and do not obey His Word, they will find themselves in a position in which the "heavens which are over your head shall be bronze, and the earth which is under you shall be iron" (v. 23). In other words, the heavens will be closed to your prayers, and nothing we attempt to do on earth will prosper. When we know what to do, we are responsible for doing it. Then, and only then, can God trust us with His yes answers and His greatest blessings.

- *How do you feel when God tells you no?*

- *What new insights do you have into why God gives us no answers?*

  _____

  _____

- *In what ways do you feel challenged in your prayer life?*

  _____

  _____

LESSON 9

PRAYING FOR OTHERS

The Bible clearly calls us to a life of prayer that includes praying for others. The apostle Paul wrote to Timothy:

> *Therefore I exhort first of all that supplications, prayers, interces-*
> *sions, and giving of thanks be made for all men, for kings and all*
> *who are in authority, that we may lead a quiet and peaceable life*
> *in all godliness and reverence. For this is good and acceptable in*
> *the sight of God our Savior, who desires all men to be saved and*
> *to come to the knowledge of the truth. . . . I desire therefore that*
> *the men pray everywhere, lifting up holy hands, without wrath and*
> *doubting.* (1 Tim. 2:1–4, 8)

This passage of Scripture tells us for whom we should pray.

We should pray for those who have authority over us. This includes political leaders, as well as judicial, social, and economic leaders. In praying for those who exert leadership in our communities and nation, we should pray that, first and foremost, they have a strong reverence for God and His commandments. We need leaders who will openly acknowledge the sovereignty of God. Then, and only then, will our leaders make decisions, pass laws, and give legal opinions that will allow us as Christians to live in peace and to have an optimum amount of opportunities for sharing the gospel.

We should pray for those who do not know the Lord or have an under-standing of the truth. We have a strong commission from God throughout the Scriptures to pray for the lost. Jesus said to His disciples, "The harvest truly is plentiful, but the laborers are few. Therefore pray the Lord of the harvest to send out laborers into His harvest" (Matt. 9:37–38). If we are to see the lost come to Christ, we must pray for the lost and pray for laborers to be sent to them. A laborer is anyone who is capable of helping a person discover the love of God that is manifested through Jesus Christ, His only Son.

Can you imagine what a different world we would live in if the vast majority of any community truly had an understanding of the truth and came to know the Lord? The crime rate would decrease, volunteer programs that benefit the needy would soar, cooperative efforts for good would abound, drug and alcohol use would diminish, businesses would become more productive, neighborhoods would be friendlier ... the list of benefits is virtually endless!

Elsewhere in the Scriptures we find two more categories of people for whom we should pray.

We should pray for the body of Christ. We need to be praying for believers who are being persecuted, those who are lukewarm in their faith, those who are cold and who are in rebellion against God and have doubts about the Scriptures, and those who are in material or physical need. Paul persistently prayed for those in the churches he helped to establish.

> *We give thanks to the God and Father of our Lord Jesus Christ, praying always for you, since we heard of your faith in Christ Jesus and of your love for all the saints. . . . We also, since the day we heard [the news of your faith], do not cease to pray for you. (Col. 1:3–4, 9)*

In his letter to the Colossians, Paul gives a clear outline of how we are to pray for our fellow believers. If you have ever wondered how to pray for other Christians—especially those you may not know very well—here is Paul's list of prayer requests. We should pray that they

• be filled with the knowledge of God's will in all wisdom and spiritual understanding.

- walk worthy of the Lord, fully pleasing Him.
- be fruitful in every good work and increase in the knowledge of God.
- be strengthened with all might, according to God's glorious power.
- have all patience and longsuffering, with joy.
- give thanks to the Father who has qualified them to be partakers of the inheritance of the saints in the light. (See Col. 1:3–12.)

In his letter to the Ephesians, Paul asked the church to pray for him "that utterance may be given to me, that I may open my mouth boldly to make known the mystery of the gospel" (Eph. 6:19). This is the same way we should pray for our pastors. We are to pray that God will show them what to say, give them boldness to say it, and help them to speak with clarity so that the gospel is no longer a mystery. We also must pray that our church leaders will stay faithful to the Lord, keep His commandments, and be given the strength to withstand the temptations and assaults of the devil.

We are to pray for those who persecute us. Jesus taught that we are to deal with our enemies in a very specific way: "Love your enemies, bless those who curse you, do good to those who hate you, and pray for those who spitefully use you and persecute you, that you may be sons of your Father in heaven" (Matt. 5:44–45).

As long as we harbor hatred, bitterness, and resentment toward our enemies, we are not trusting the Lord to deal with them as *He* wills, but rather, only to deal with them as *we* will. When we pray for our enemies with an attitude of forgiveness and love, then God is free to deal with them with His omniscient, omnipotent love. He can cleanse their hearts. He can heal them and make them whole— that includes, of course, their having a good relationship with us.

The benefit of all these prayers, the Bible says, is that we may be allowed to live Christian lives that will flourish, prosper, and be fulfilling. If our persecutors are silenced, our leaders are godly, our churches are led by Spirit-filled men and women, and the lost are being won to Christ, then the body of Christ will expand and develop in wonderful ways. We truly will be allowed to live quiet lives in godliness and reverence.

Furthermore, *we* change even as we pray for change in the lives of others. Often as we pray for others, God shows us ways in which we need to adjust our attitudes, move toward others with love, or soften our behavior. We must remain open to God's dealing with us, even as we pray for our enemies.

- *How do you feel when you pray for others?*

_____

_____

- *In what ways are you being challenged in your prayer life?*

_____

_____

- *What new insights do you have into these Scripture passages about how you should pray for others?*

  1 Timothy 2:1–3, 8

  _____

  _____

  Matthew 9:37–38

  _____

  _____

  Colossians 1:3–12

  _____

  _____

  Ephesians 6:18–19

  _____

  _____

  Matthew 5:44–45

  _____

  _____

- *Have you had an experience in which you prayed for God to change another person and He required you to change as part of the process?*

_____

_____

Principles for Effective Intercession for Others

Each of us has had an experience in which we have prayed for other people and have not seen any results. When that happens, it's easy to get discouraged. Rather than give up on our intercession, we are wise to review our lives to see if we need to alter something in our own lives so that our prayers will be more effective. Here are six key principles for effective intercession:

1. Our prayers must flow from a heart filled with love, compassion, and forgiveness. Our prayers are not effective if we have hearts filled with bitterness, resentment, or anger. In praying for others, make your first prayer a prayer for yourself that you might have God's love and compassion for others, and that you truly might forgive them fully.

2. We must recognize that our prayers are the link between another person's need and God's inexhaustible resources. As we pray with a pure heart for another person's need, God acts on that person's behalf. The responsibility to pray is an awesome one. He expects us to see needs and to pray about them. When we do not pray, others remain in need. The problem may not be their lack of faith or lack of relationship with the Father as much as it is our lack of prayer.

As you pray, ask the Lord to reveal to you the true needs of a person, not just the superficial or symptomatic needs. Ask Him also to reveal to you the greatness of His love and power and desire to meet those needs and to bring the person to wholeness.

3. We must identify with the need of the other person. Compassion is feeling the full depth of another's need. We must be willing in our compassion to get under and help carry the spiritual burden of the other person. This is one of the main reasons we must pray that the Lord will reveal the deepest level of need in the person's life. When we see people as truly hurting, bleeding, and agonizing on the inside—when we see them with the eyes of Jesus and we recognize that we, too, have those same needs at our deepest spiritual level—our compassion is released. We pray with a new degree of understanding and depth of emotion.

4. *We must always desire the highest good in another person's life.* The person's highest good may not be what the person in need is requesting, or what we at first think to pray. When we say to the Father, "I want what's best for this person," we must never add an "if," "and," or "but" to our prayer. We must take our hands off the person and let God put His hands on him or her. This is very difficult to do, especially for parents who are praying for their children.

God may or may not reveal to us what His highest good is going to be for another person, but we can make it our prayer nonetheless. We do not need to know the full potential for blessing in another person's life in order to trust God to bring it to pass. Ultimately, God's highest good is *wholeness.* Jesus said repeatedly to those who were brought to Him, "Be made whole." Wholeness includes vibrancy and life in every domain: spirit, mind, body, emotions, relationships, and finances.

5. *We must be willing to be part of the answer in meeting the other person's need.* When you pray for another person, and you are not willing to be used by God to meet that person's need, God will not hear your prayer. You are actually voicing your prayer with a desire for isolation and separation—which is self-centeredness—not with a desire truly to be a part of the greater body of Christ. Jesus touched lepers, the unclean, the desperately sick, and the dead. He never backed away from people who came to Him in need or passed them on to someone else for healing and deliverance. We are to follow His example.

6. *We must be willing to persevere in prayer.* We must keep on praying for others, regardless of whether we see immediate results. The longer we pray for a person with compassion and a desire to see God make that person whole, the more tightly our hearts will be knit to him or her. Prayer binds us together with a spiritual glue that is stronger than anything humankind can ever create. It is a bond that will last into eternity.

- *Recall a time in your life in which you experienced great need. How did you feel? How did you want others to pray for you?*

What the Word Says

These things I command you, that you love one another. (John 15:17)

The prayer of faith will save the sick, and the Lord will raise him up. And if he has committed sins, he will be forgiven. Confess your trespasses to one another, and pray for one another,
that you may be healed. (James 5:15–16)

My God shall supply all your need according to His riches in glory by Christ Jesus. (Phil. 4:19)

Jesus had compassion and touched their eyes. (Matt. 20:34)

Love suffers long and is kind . . . bears all things, believes all things, hopes all things, endures all things. (1 Cor. 13:4, 7)

What the Word Says to Me

- *Have you ever had an experience of genuine, compassionate, loving prayer for others? How did you feel? What were the results?*

- *What new insights do you have into God's call to pray for others?*

• *In what ways are you being challenged in your prayer life?*

_____

_____

A Challenge to Pray for Others

I challenge you today to ask God to reveal to you three people for whom you should pray. Ask Him to show you three people who are suffering great pain or heartache. Ask Him to give you His love and compassion for those people and to show you ways in which you might help carry their spiritual and emotional burdens, as well as ways in which you might be of assistance to them in practical ways.

Then, begin to pray for them. Ask God to make them whole, beginning with their deepest needs. It is not enough to know *how* to pray for others. What is required of us is that we actually do so.

TIME TO PRAY OR TIME TO ACT?

Jesus was a Man of intense and frequent prayer. The Gospels have numerous accounts of Jesus withdrawing to pray. Prayer is a thread that ran throughout His life and ministry.

The disciples were men of prayer, as were members of the early church. When Peter was imprisoned by Herod, "constant prayer was offered to God for him by the church" (Acts 12:5).

The apostle Paul repeatedly stated that we must *always* be in prayer: "For God is my witness, . . . that without ceasing I make mention of you always in my prayers" (Rom. 1:9); "I thank my God upon every remembrance of you, always in every prayer of mine making request for you all with joy" (Phil. 1:3–4); "Pray without ceasing" (1 Thess. 5:17).

As you read the New Testament looking for references to prayer, you are going to find them popping up from the pages frequently and almost insistently—they not only tell us about prayer but compel us to pray. Prayer is the undergirding foundation for all good works, all miracles, and all spiritual fruitfulness. *God desires to have a praying people!*

However, the Scriptures state that there are times when we are *not* to pray. Instead, we are to act. Prayer must never be a substitute for speaking to others and acting toward others as the Holy Spirit desires. We must never hide behind a shield of prayer, saying to God, in effect, "I would obey You, but I'm too busy praying." Our lives are to be in balance: pray and do. Trust and obey. Hear and follow. The Scriptures plainly tell us that we are to be active doers of God's Word. (See James 1:22; John 13:17.)

One of the best examples of this in the Bible is in Joshua 7:1–13:

> *But the children of Israel committed a trespass regarding the accursed things, for Achan . . . took of the accursed things; so the anger of the LORD burned against the children of Israel.*
>
> *Now Joshua sent men from Jericho to Ai . . . and spoke to them, saying, "Go up and spy out the country." So the men went up and spied out Ai. And they returned to Joshua and said to him, "Do not let all the people go up, but let about two or three thousand men go up and attack Ai. Do not weary all the people there, for the people of Ai are few." So about three thousand men went up there from the people, but they fled before the men of Ai. And the men of Ai struck down about thirty-six men, for they chased them from before the gate as far as Shebarim, and struck them down on the descent; therefore the hearts of the people melted and became like water.*
>
> *Then Joshua tore his clothes, and fell to the earth on his face before the ark of the LORD until evening, he and the elders of Israel; and they put dust on their heads. And Joshua said, "Alas, Lord GOD, why have You brought this people over the Jordan at all— to deliver us into the hand of the Amorites, to destroy us? Oh, that we had been content, and dwelt on the other side of the Jordan! O Lord, what shall I say when Israel turns its back before its enemies? For the Canaanites and all the inhabitants of the land will hear it, and surround us, and cut off our name from the earth. Then what will You do for Your great name?"*
>
> *So the LORD said to Joshua: "Get up! Why do you lie thus on your face? Israel has sinned, and they have also transgressed My covenant which I commanded them. For they have even taken some of the accursed things, and have both stolen and deceived; and they have also put it among their own stuff. Therefore the children of Israel could not stand before their enemies, but turned their backs before their enemies, because they have become doomed to destruction. Neither will I be with you anymore, unless you destroy the accursed from among you. Get up, sanctify the people, and say, 'Sanctify yourselves for tomorrow, because thus says the LORD God of Israel: "There is an accursed thing in your midst, O Israel; you*

cannot stand before your enemies until you take away the accursed thing from among you."[11]

Immediately after God had given the Israelites a great victory at Jericho, Joshua sent men to spy out Ai. Although Ai wasn't nearly the city that Jericho was, the Israelites were soundly defeated. It was a serious setback that caused grief and fear to fill the Israelite camp.

What was the difference in the approaches of the Israelites to Jericho and Ai? First, God gave Joshua a mandate to defeat Jericho and accompanied it by a promise that He would give Jericho into Joshua's hand. Furthermore, God gave Joshua the military strategy by which the victory was to be won. (See Josh. 6.) The victory was God's, and He received full glory for it.

When God gives instructions, He is very precise. He doesn't deal with generalities. He uses specific methods for specific circumstances. Jericho is the only city in the Scriptures that was taken by the Israelites, because the priests and the people carried the ark of the covenant around it once a day for six days and then seven times on the seventh day.

God no doubt had a battle plan for Ai, but Joshua didn't wait to receive it. Joshua sent out spies just as he had for Jericho, and when they came back with a report that Ai could easily be taken, Joshua dispatched a few thousand men without consulting God. He relied solely on prideful human opinion.

- *Recall an experience in your life in which you were facing a major challenge or decision and you did not pray and receive God's guidance before proceeding. What was the result in the short term? The long term?*

_____

_____

Second, God had commanded as a part of the victory over Jericho that the people of Israel not touch the "accursed things"—items that were considered unclean according to the Law, including the personal effects of the people of Jericho. They were only to take the silver, gold, bronze, and iron vessels for the treasury of the house of the Lord, and burn the rest. Joshua gave very clear instructions to the men of Israel: "By all means abstain from the accursed things, lest you become accursed when you take of the accursed things, and make the camp of Israel a curse, and trouble it" (Josh. 6:18).

Achan did not obey. He brought accursed things into the camp, including a beautiful Babylonian garment. He also took two hundred shekels of silver and wedges of gold for himself. He buried them in the ground inside his tent.

Had Joshua sought God's face before moving against Ai, I have no doubt that God would have revealed to Joshua what Achan had done. The problem could and should have been resolved before any assault was made on Ai. If it had been, I also have no doubt that the Israelites would have been successful a second time, again without any loss of Israelite life.

- *In looking back over some of your heartaches and failures, is there a time you can recall when something needed to be changed or corrected before you took a specific action? Do you believe the Lord would have revealed that to you if you had prayed about the situation?*

_____

_____

- *What new insights do you have into this passage from Joshua 7:1–13?*

_____

_____

The Importance of Asking the Right Question

When the men of Israel returned in defeat, Joshua turned immediately to prayer. He tore his garment, an act of grief, and he fell on his face in humiliation before the ark of the covenant until nightfall. All of the elders joined him in this act. Joshua cried out to God, "Why did You do this to us?"

Joshua asked the wrong question. It is a question that many of us ask when trouble strikes us. Our first impulse is to blame God for the tragedy or problem that is overwhelming us. We cry out, "Why?

Why me? What did I do to deserve this? Why did You allow me to get in this mess?" Although these questions may be our initial responses, they are the wrong questions to ask. The appropriate questions to ask are: "What did I do that was wrong? How did I get into this mess? What can I do to correct this situation?"

Sometimes we need to change a habit or correct a bad attitude. We may need to confront our own sin and error. In the vast majority of cases, God is not at all the cause for our trouble or need. We human beings are at fault, either collectively or individually.

When Joshua had ceased pouring out his hurt, frustration, and questioning to God, God said, "Get up! Why are you lying on your face? Israel has sinned and that is the reason for your defeat."

When we go to God in prayer, we must be willing to hear what God says to us. Often, people go to God in prayer about a situation, voice their petition, and never stop to hear back from God. In fact, they never even give it a thought that God might want to say something to them. We must wait when we voice our petitions to God to hear His response.

This is especially true when we are praying in the aftermath of a setback or defeat in our lives. It is also vitally important that we do this anytime we find ourselves blaming God for our troubles. We must be willing to listen for His explanation, which is very often a correction.

Once the Lord reveals to us what we need to correct, the time for prayer has ended. There is nothing more to be said—no excuses, no attempt to justify what we have done or what has happened. We must accept what the Lord says and immediately move to obey Him. Our obedience may include asking Him to forgive us and to help us to obey Him in the future. But our actions of obedience must follow quickly. There are usually amends to be made or specific actions to be taken that will help right the wrong.

In Joshua's case, he rose early the next morning, organized Israel by tribes, and discovered who had taken the accursed things. He moved quickly to correct the problem. In fact, he resolved the situation before the day ended.

After the sin had been cleansed from the camp, the Lord said to Joshua,

Do not be afraid, nor be dismayed; take all the people of war with you, and arise, go up to Ai. See, I have given into your hand the king of Ai, his people, his city, and his land. And you shall do to Ai and its king as you did to Jericho and its king. Only its spoil and its cattle you shall take as booty for yourselves. Lay an ambush for the city behind it. (Joshua 8:1–2)

When Joshua did as God commanded, the people were successful. No Israelite lives were lost, the city was brought to desolation, and there was great bounty added to the camp of the Israelites.

There are times when we find it much easier to pray about our sins than to turn our back on them. It is easier to pray for another person than to do something practical to help that person. It is easier to pray for our relationship with another person than to take steps to make amends or to reconcile. It is easier to pray about our indebtedness than to curb our spending habits. But at these times God calls us to get up off our knees and deal with the problems that we have created for ourselves. Then, and only then, will He bless us.

• *In what ways are you being challenged in your prayer life?*

_____

_____

Four Principles for Deciding Whether to Pray or Act

The story from Joshua gives us four key principles that we can use to test whether we should keep praying or start acting:

First, there is a time to wait before God in prayer and a time to act. The time to wait is when we do not have a clear understanding, direction, or mandate from God to act. Until we know what to do regarding a specific circumstance, need, problem, relationship, or opportunity, we should remain in prayer.

The time to act is when the Lord reveals to us anything that needs to be corrected or changed in our lives. Sometimes the change is a new behavior we need to develop or a new step we are to take.

Second, blaming God in prayer is a waste of time. Anytime you are holding God responsible for your troubles, you are in error. God does not do bad things *to* people. God does good things *for* people. He may have allowed your own error or sin to result in something bad in your life, but He has allowed it so that you might learn from it, correct the situation, and move forward to greater blessing. He may have allowed a tragic circumstance to occur in your life, but He has a plan for good to come from it as you yield your life to Him and trust Him to use this tragedy for a much greater and higher blessing in your life and the lives of those around you.

Third, when God shows you an error that needs to be corrected, correct it immediately. You may need to ask the Lord how and when you should take specific actions, especially if someone else is involved, but take very specific steps to correct your error immediately.

Certainly we can pray as we take the steps that God has ordered. We don't have to be on our knees or in a secluded place to pray. Our prayers don't cease, but our period of "waiting" on the Lord should end at the moment God reveals to us what we are to do. No excuses, and no delays.

Fourth, don't substitute prayer for action. Do not compound your error by thinking that you can "pray the problem away." If God has revealed to you an error that involves your job, your marriage, your children, your church relationships, your friendships, your health, your finances . . . those errors will not be resolved fully or solely by prayer. His command to us is, "Deal with this!"

We may not be able to achieve full reconciliation, arrive at a total solution, or meet the entirety of need through one conversation or one action. We may need to deal with the problem, and then deal further with the problem, and then deal even further with the problem. Most problems are not created in a day or resolved in a day. Our prayer as we deal with the situation is to be constant: "Lord, give me courage to do this, give me wisdom to know how to do this, give me strength to persist in doing this." This kind of prayer complements our action; it is not a substitute for action.

God requires us to take initiative. We must have a zeal for doing what is right in His eyes if God's work in us is going to continue and if His kingdom is going to continue to be expand. He asks us to pray so He can guide and direct our initiative, but He expects us to work, speak, exert, give, share . . . in a word, *do.*

If we fail to deal with a problem after God reveals it to us, we are cheating ourselves of future success. The roadblock to our success doesn't disappear or vanish. It remains until we attend to it. How much better to act on it quickly than to delay or to turn away and deny that the roadblock exists.

What the Word Says	What the Word Says to Me
I will say to God, "Do not condemn me; Show me why You contend with me. . . . Seek for my iniquity And search out my sin." (Job 10:2, 6)	_____
Show me Your ways, O LORD; Teach me Your paths. Lead me in Your truth and teach me, For You are the God of my salvation; On You I wait all the day. (Ps. 25:4–5)	_____
Therefore my heart is glad, and my glory rejoices; My flesh also will rest in hope. For You will not leave my soul in Sheol, Nor will You allow Your Holy One to see corruption. You will show me the path of life. (Ps. 16:9–11)	_____

- *What new insights do you have into the balance between prayer and action in God's Word?*

_____

_____

- *In what ways are you being challenged in your prayer life?*

_____

_____

Opening the Way to Future Success

When we act on the problems that the Lord reveals to us in prayer, we take one step closer to realizing the full potential that the Lord has placed within us. We come closer to receiving more of the abundant blessings He has for us. We grow deeper in our relationship with the Lord, for we experience anew His mercy and loving forgiveness. And we have greater insight into the righteousness, justice, and perfection of God. We see with renewed insight the glory that belongs to God alone. He is the One who is refining us and perfecting us, teaching us and training us to be His people. How blessed we are to have a relationship with Him! How awesome to know that we can come to God in prayer and always, always, *always* be welcomed with loving and everlasting arms, even if we hear words of correction from Him.

CONCLUSION

A LIFE OF PRAYER

God repeatedly calls His people to come to Him. We first come to Him when we recognize our sinfulness, casting ourselves on His mercy to forgive us our sins and to impart to us His Holy Spirit.

Daily we are to come to Him for guidance in making choices and decisions, for forgiveness for our sins, for correction and teaching regarding our errors, for deliverance from evil, and to voice our petitions for protection and provision. On a daily basis the Holy Spirit imparts to us the ability to live godly lives.

Our relationship with our heavenly Father grows and deepens as we enter into a life of daily prayer. We can devise no other means to this growth through our own strength and ability. God has made no other provision for it. *Prayer is the means to intimacy with God.*

I once heard someone say, "Prayer is a laboratory class. It isn't a theory-based course. It is a practicum." The most important lessons about prayer that you can ever learn are ones that you will learn by praying.

I encourage you today to begin, or to renew, your commitment to talk with God on a daily basis. Listen closely to Him. Hear His thoughts and plans for you. They are thoughts and plans for your good. Delight in your relationship with the Lord. He delights in you.